MICHELIN

VENICE

— in your pocket —

PHOTOGRAPH CREDITS
Travel Library title page, 5, 9, 44, 73, 95, 99; Travel
Library/Stuart Black 38, 75, 102, 105, 117, 125; Travel
Library/Daniel Cilia back cover, 63, 97, 113; Travel
Library/Philip Enticknap front cover, 7, 11, 23, 25, 29,
41, 43, 45, 51, 56, 61, 69, 71, 76, 82, 88, 93, 104, 107,
109, 120, 123; Bridgeman Art Library 12, 13, 15, 17, 33,
34, 35, 37, 52, 59, 90; Greg Evans International/Greg
Balfour Evans; 101; Sarah Quill/Archivio Veneziano 19,
21, 26, 30, 46, 47, 48, 50, 54, 57, 60, 64, 65, 66, 67, 68,
70, 77, 78, 79, 80, 81, 84, 85, 86, 87, 91, 100, 103; The
Venice in Peril Fund/Sarah Quill (Enquiries and contri-
butions to: Suite 2-3 Morley House, 314-322 Regent
Street, London W1R 5AB; tel 0171 636 6138) 27.

*Front cover: Santa Maria della Salute; back cover: Carnival
mask; title page: view to St Mark's Square and the Doges'
Palace*

While every effort is made to ensure that the information in this guide is as accurate and up-to-date
as possible, detailed information is constantly changing. The publishers cannot accept responsibility
for any consequences resulting from changes in information, errors or omissions.

MANUFACTURE FRANÇAISE DES PNEUMATIQUES MICHELIN
Société en commandite par actions au capital de 2 000 000 000 de francs
Place des Carmes-Déchaux – 63 Clermont-Ferrand (France)
R.C.S. Clermont-Fd 855 200 507
© Michelin et Cie. Propriétaires-Éditeurs 1996
Dêpôt légal Avril 96 – ISBN 2-06-650901-9 – ISSN: en cours

Printed in the EU 3-96

CONTENTS

INTRODUCTION

La Serenissima Repubblica

No one knows when the Venice was first referred to as 'the Most Serene Republic', but by the 14C it had become a recognized epithet. Many Italian cities had high-flown titles but this, unlike most, was exactly descriptive, for, throughout the long centuries from the fall of the Roman Empire to the Napoleonic conquest of Italy, Venice alone of the cities of Italy knew internal tranquillity – serenity. No bloody revolutions; no brutal repressions; no merciless sackings by conquering armies; no jumped-up strutting dictators; no cowering people. The Venetians paid a price for that serenity (*see* p.17-18), but the fact that they paid that price for well over a thousand years shows they were happy to do so.

The phrase 'La Serenissima' could apply to the government, to the people in general, or even to the physical city. The feminine form of the word was particularly appropriate, for Venetians saw their city as a beautiful woman. Tiepolo's great painting in the Doges' Palace *Venice Receiving the Gifts of the Sea* shows Neptune offering a cornucopia to a proud and beautiful woman, her hair dressed in the height of fashion (*see* p.59).

It seems likely that this wondrous city is approaching the end of its days. Not in our time, certainly, but sooner or later the sea which created it will reclaim it, leaving perhaps its major monuments fossilized as museum pieces. But today, to wander through the quiet city shortly after dawn, before the coaches arrive, to watch at noon Henry James's 'hundred nameless reflections' on the canals, or the moonlight

Dawn falls on Venice, the serene city.

bathing the Salute as Stendhal saw it, is to realize that Venice's sunset is different from, but as splendid as, her high noon. No longer a republic, she is still the world's most serene city.

HOW TO USE THIS GUIDE

This guide is divided into four main sections:

Background sets the scene, beginning with a summary of Venice's colourful history and its geographical context, including a look at the problems of erosion to Venice's canals. Finally, there is a section on Art and Architecture, with a special feature on Titian.

Exploring Venice opens with a view of the city as seen by travellers through the ages. A list of the top ten sights which should be on everyone's holiday checklist follows. There are then four detailed itineraries exploring the beauties of Venice and its surrounding islands. The tours cover: the heart of the city around St Mark's Square, a trip along the Grand Canal, things to see outside the city centre and finally, a tour of the islands of the lagoon. A guide to the Museums and Galleries of Venice rounds off this section.

Enjoying Your Visit provides friendly, no-nonsense advice on day-to-day holiday activities which can make the difference between a good holiday and a great one – eating out, shopping, entertainment and nightlife, as well as details of the famous Venetian Carnival and other festivals.

A-Z Factfinder is an easy-to-use reference section packed with useful information, covering everything you may need to know on your visit, from tipping to transport, from using the telephone to tourist information offices. A word of warning: opening hours and telephone numbers frequently change, so be sure to double check first.

The Campanile, church and monastery of San Giorgio Maggiore mirrors the Campanile of St Mark's opposite.

HISTORY

The People of the Mud Flats

The collapse of the Roman empire in the 5C AD brought the barbarians howling into what is now Italy, entering from the north-east. Italians scattered in their path, some of them seeking refuge on the dozens of small, flat islands dotted around a coastal lagoon. Temporary encampments were thrown up, followed by more solid buildings, placed on wooden piles driven deep in the mud – a method of construction which was to prove astonishingly durable: as late as 1631 the immense church of the Salute, weighing thousands of tons, was built on such close-packed piles.

Each of the little islets was independent of its neighbours but, like seamen on a ship, they found co-operation was essential to fight off the common enemy, the sea. From that need rose the paradoxical Venetian character: all men equal but subordinate to the common good. All other Italian cities, even the proud republic of Florence, eventually fell to the despotic rule of one man or one family. This has never happened throughout Venice's history.

The mainland continued in turbulence as the rich cities of Italy fell to foreign conquerors or fought each other for dominance. No one thought it worthwhile to harass the poor, but remarkably pugnacious, fishermen on their muddy islets, and the Venetians were left alone to build their floating city. They had two vital products literally on their doorstep – fish and salt — and, trading with these, they launched one of the world's great commercial empires.

Gradually, the Venetians concentrated on the group of islands known as the Rialto (derived from the words *rivo alto*, 'high embankment'). It made sense to build bridges between the islands and to fill in the narrower channels and so enlarge the land area. Inevitably, physical compactness led to social compactness. It is not known exactly when this chance-gathered group of refugees became a city. Tradition has it that they declared themselves a community at exactly noon on Friday 25 March 421, and though this is suspiciously exact it is probably fairly reliable. In 697 they elected one of their number who was given the Latin title of *Dux*. This is usually translated as

The broad span of the Grand Canal, looking towards Santa Maria della Salute.

'duke', but the original meaning of 'leader' would be a better word, for that is what the embryonic citizens intended. The Venetian dialect turned 'dux' into 'doge' and so created an office which would last for more than 1 100 years.

The City-State

Until the 19C 'Italy' was not one country but was composed of a mosaic of sovereign city-states, which grew fewer and larger as the stronger absorbed the weaker. Of them all, Venice was the only one that remained a republic.

However, it was not a republic which would be recognized in the 20C. Indeed, it far more resembled Orwell's *1984*, where a small elite governed the rest but were themselves under intense supervision. The only people who had votes were the nobility, those whose names were inscribed in the famous Golden Book – about 2 000 adult males out of a population of some 120 000. These formed the **Maggior Consiglio,** the Great Council.

The nobility themselves were under the scrutiny of the **Council of Ten** and the three Inquisitors, known simply as the **Council of Three**. These had literally life-and-death powers over every Venetian: as the saying of the time went, 'The Ten control the torture chamber: the Three the grave.' **Casanova** was one of those who fell into their power – not for his amatory activities but for a crime against the state: he persuaded two young noblemen to become freemasons. He was sentenced to five years' imprisonment in the Doges' Palace, but managed to escape and left a vivid account of his experience. His cell is still shown to visitors.

The Doge

At the apex of Venetian society was the paradoxical figure of the doge: paradoxical, because although he was elected for life, and was loaded with honours and power – a powerful doge could alter the history of the city – he was also regarded with deep and continual suspicion by his fellow nobles lest he develop ideas of turning an elected office into a position of personal power. It was more than his life was worth to give grounds to that suspicion, as shown by the grim statistics of the dogeship: by the early 15C seven doges had been assassinated, one beheaded, twelve had abdicated under pressure and two were deposed.

The election of a doge involved a complex process of alternating lotteries and nominations. At a special ceremony in the basilica a young boy, chosen at random from

A close-up of some of the magnificent mosaics adorning the terrace of St Mark's Basilica.

the congregation, took 30 names from a golden urn. These were reduced to nine by lot, and they in turn chose 40, who were reduced to 12... the process continuing until an electoral college emerged who finally chose the doge. Yet even this system was capable of manipulation, and the Council of Ten were utterly merciless in their reaction against any doge suspected of monarchical ambition, as the story of Francesco Foscari demonstrated.

The Two Foscari

The tragedy of **Francesco Foscari** and his son **Jacopo**, 'the two Foscari', is one of the great set-pieces of Venetian history, attracting a poet of Byron's status. Foscari's

Portrait of the Doge Francesco Foscari (1460) by Lazzaro Bastiani (Correr Museum).

election in 1423 was a close-run thing. Although a noble he was poor, and on election threw himself with gusto into the business of being Doge. His wife, now the Dogaressa, was brought to the palace in the Bucintoro (the ducal barge) like a queen. It so happened that the superb murals in the Council Hall (Sala del Maggior Consiglio) were completed in his first year of office. He opened the Hall with great ceremony, and probably most ordinary citizens thought that the murals were his personal contribution. During his reign, the city began to blaze forth in its Renaissance splendour, for much of which he took credit. He placed his statue with the Lion of St Mark over the entrance to the Doges' Palace. He married his son into the Contarini, one of the oldest families in that city of long-established patricians. He received the Emperor on equal terms.

But the Ten were watching and began a cat-and-mouse campaign which went on for

Gentile Bellini's portrayal of a grand procession in St Mark's Square (Academy of Fine Arts).

12 years. They exiled his son and compelled him, as Doge, to sign the instrument of exile. It broke the old man, then 84, and he pleaded to be allowed to abdicate. The Ten refused: no Doge could abdicate without the consent of the Great Council. Then came news of Jacopo's death – and the Ten demanded Francesco's resignation. The demand was couched in terms that can be read either as a heartlessly cynical exercise, or as an example of the Venetian veneration of the State and of the office of doge which symbolized it. The Ten deplored that their 'most illustrious Prince' was incapable by reason of age and infirmity of carrying out his office and should 'as a good prince and Father of his Country, resign'. With a return of his old spirit, he refused. The Ten then resorted to naked threats: if he did not go he would be thrown out, his property confiscated and his pension rescinded. He bowed to the inevitable and died a week later.

Even then the Ten had not finished. His widow wanted a private funeral but the Ten insisted that, as an ex-doge, his body belonged to the State and must be given a State funeral. It was taken away, despite her passionate protests.

Queen of the Seas

In 1204 there took place an event which indelibly stained Venice's honour – but put her finally on the road to empire. Under Doge **Enrico Dandolo,** over 80 years of age and almost blind, the Venetians tricked the gullible French and Normans of the Fourth Crusade into attacking the Christian city of Constantinople. In a way, Venice was attacking her foster-mother, the origin of the

Byzantine culture, but for Dandolo the city had become a rival. The conquest of Constantinople gave Venice vital footholds on the islands and coast of the eastern Mediterranean, among them Crete, the Peloponnese and Cyprus.

'Once did she hold the gorgeous East in fee,' Wordsworth wrote of Venice, but she did so for the most humdrum and practical reasons. Trade was the main interest of the Serenissima, and she acquired an empire solely to advance that interest. And it was to the east that she looked, stimulated by the extraordinary experiences of **Marco Polo** and his father and uncle. In 1292, they returned after nearly 25 years in Cathay (China) to find that nobody recognized them. They staged a dramatic unveiling in their palace, stripping off their worn-out oriental clothes, from which poured emeralds, rubies and pearls. Venetian trade

The Grand Canal in the 18C by Canaletto.

was essentially luxury trade.

The Venetians divided the world into two: the *Stato del Mare* and the *Stato della Terra Ferma*. They were thoroughly at home in the State of the Sea but regarded the State of the Mainland with suspicion. They wanted nothing to do with it. Indeed, it was Francesco Foscari's declared policy to expand the state to the mainland which probably led to his downfall. But gradually, as the embattled city-states of Italy brought their wars closer and closer to Venice, she had to react in self-defence, particularly as the powerful dukes of Milan remorselessly extended their eastern frontier. Venice acquired Verona, Vicenza and Padua not by military conquest but by negotiation: these cities preferred Venice to Milan, as it allowed them to keep their constitutions, with Venice controlling and co-ordinating finance and defence.

A European Power

Willy-nilly the Serenissima was now a land-power, drawn into European battles. She was supremely well equipped in the diplomatic and financial fields. Her ambassadors knew every detail of life in the countries to which they were appointed. When there was a threatened Huguenot rising in France, the Venetian Senate was better informed about their military potential than was the French government. Despite the Senate's dislike of land warfare, Venice was one of the few powers able to control mercenaries, **Carmagnola's** fate being a powerful incentive to loyalty (*see* p.20).

The republic's influence on the mainland grew so great that an international alliance came into being to bring it down. The so-

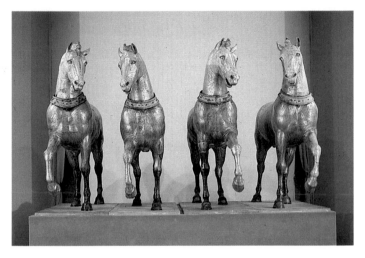

called **'Holy League'**, signed in 1508 in Cambrai, included the Pope, the kings of Spain and France and the dukes of Ferrara and Savoy. Venice survived, her diplomats exploiting with consummate skill the inevitable rifts that appeared among the ill-assorted allies.

Her veteran diplomats, however, failed her at last when faced with the 26-year-old Corsican soldier, **Napoleon Bonaparte.** By the 18C the thousand-year-old republic was tiring and had almost, it seemed, lost the will to live. Austria and France pressed the Senate to choose between them in their quarrel: the Senate preferred a lukewarm neutrality, incurring Napoleon's wrath. 'I shall be an Attila to Venice!' he snarled in his thick Corsican accent, and threatened to bombard the city. Venice deserved better than almost the last recorded remark of the last doge, **Lodovico Manin**. Trembling, he

The four famous bronze horses which once adorned St Mark's Basilica are now housed in the Museum of the Basilica.

whimpered, 'Tonight there will be no safety for us, not even in our own beds.' The terrified Great Council met for the last time on Friday 12 May 1797 and voted their own dissolution. The world's oldest republic died at its own hands.

The Defence of the City

Other Italian cities encased themselves in immense walls of stone. Venice's defences were wooden, the deadly **Venetian fighting galley** which dominated the Mediterranean until the coming of the great ships of the French, Spanish, Dutch and English navies in the 17C. Manned by free men, frequently nobles, the galley was also employed as a trading vessel, carrying goods of small bulk and high value, such as spices and silk.

All ships of whatever class belonged to the State, and to create and maintain their fleet the rulers of the Serenissima developed what is certainly Europe's, and possibly the world's, first major industrial complex. In 1104 on the north-east of the city they founded a shipyard, to which they gave the odd Arabic name of *dar as-sin'a* or 'house of industry'. The Venetian dialect turned the word into *arsenale* and so gave a word to all European languages. At its peak in the 16C the Arsenal was employing 16 000 men in a method of mass production that predated Henry Ford's by many centuries. It was calculated that the Arsenal could produce a fully equipped ship in 100 days. A Spanish observer described how one of these galleys was fitted out for sea. 'Out came a galley towed by a boat and from the windows [of the buildings lining the canal] they handed to the occupants from one the cordage, from another the arms and from another the ballisters and mortars and so from all sides everything that was required, and when the galley had reached the end of the street [the canal] all the men required were on board and she was equipped from end to end.' The entire operation was completed in less than two hours. It was the Venetian galley, some 65m (180ft) long, with a ramming beak of an additional 7m (20ft),

The monumental gateway to the Arsenal, the shipbuilding centre of Venice in the 12C, has baroque statues and lions of Greek origin.

7m (20ft) wide and heavily armed with cannons, that formed the backbone of the Christian fleet at the **Battle of Lepanto** which saved Europe from the Turks in 1571.

The city's intimate relationship with the sea was formalized with the ritual of the **Wedding of the Sea**, first celebrated in 1177. On each Ascension Day the Doge was rowed in the splendid state barge, the Bucintoro, out into the Adriatic, where he cast a gold ring into the sea with the words 'We wed thee, o Sea, as a sign of true and perpetual dominion,' ('But you've been cuckolded by the Turk!' a French ambassador mocked on news of a resounding naval defeat for Venice). The ceremony fell into disuse, but was revived in the 1970s as a somewhat self-conscious occasion for the tourist trade.

The Condottieri

All-powerful at sea, Venice deeply distrusted engagements on land. But, as the battles on the mainland pressed ever closer, the Serenissima was obliged to wage land campaigns to protect its territory. Since the city had never needed to develop an army, there was no alternative but to employ mercenaries, the most uncertain of all military means. Self-governing armies thousands strong, they owed no allegiance to anyone or any country, except to their *condottiero*, so called because he negotiated the condotta or contract with the new employer, and his prime interest was to gain the best terms with the least danger for himself and his men.

The problem that Venice faced was vividly illustrated by the conduct of the famous condottiero **Francesco Carmagnola**. He had been fighting for the Duke of Milan, and

The Colleoni Monument, by Andrea del Verrocchio, stands majestic in the Campo SS Giovanni e Paolo.

switched allegiance to Venice after a quarrel with him. At first he served his new employer well and was rewarded with a splendid palace on the Grand Canal. But then, in 1427, the powers of the Serenissima grew convinced that he was contemplating switching back. There was no way a condottiero could be arrested while in the field among thousands of his men, but a typically Venetian trick solved the problem. He was invited to a private dinner with the Doge in his palace, which he attended unarmed and unaccompanied – and was seized. 'I am lost,' he cried, as he was dragged away. He was tortured, confessed, and was condemned.

But he had been a great servant of the State and the Venetians set great store by ceremony and protocol. He was allowed – or rather, obliged – to wear the splendid costume of scarlet cloak and crimson tunic that betokened his rank. The cloak decently hid the fact that his hands were tied behind him, and only those close at hand could see that a wooden gag had been thrust into his mouth to prevent treasonable utterances as he was led to the 'usual place' of execution between the columns on the Piazzetta. His last sight on earth would have been the waters of the lagoon under the westering sun and then the marble pavement under his knees.

His successor, **Bartolomeo Colleoni**, was more honourable, or perhaps wiser. He actually turned down an offer from Louis XII of France which would have doubled his pay as Venice's Captain General. The Serenissima repaid him with a signal honour (for a sound financial reason). After his death his executors were allowed to raise a statue to him – unheard of before for a private citizen. The sculptor chosen was **Andrea del Verrocchio** and the **Colleoni Monument** in the Campo SS Giovanni e Paolo, completed in 1496, is one of the great ornaments of the city.

GEOGRAPHY

The city lies in the centre of a broad, shallow **lagoon** that in many places is only waist-deep. Channels have been dredged to allow large ships to enter the industrial port of Maghera on the mainland; other channels are marked by poles, once wooden but now some are concrete. On the east the lagoon is protected by two long, low, narrow spits of land, the Lido and Pellestrina, both of which are inhabited. In the 18C their natural protection was enhanced by massive stone seawalls, which still play a vital role in the lagoon's defence.

The historic centre consists of over one hundred **islands**, linked by hundreds of bridges. The flat-bottomed **gondola**, which can spin on its axis, was evolved to navigate the canals, many of which turn at right angles. Today, gondolas operate almost exclusively for tourists, most water traffic being by motorboat or **water-buses** (*vaporetti*). Gondolas still operate as public ferries (*traghetti*) crossing the Grand Canal.

The city is divided into six regions or

The splendid view across to Santa Maria della Salute, from the Campanile, San Giorgio Maggiore.

sestieri. San Marco is the most fashionable – and expensive – and contains the major historical buildings. The other five regions are San Polo (the centre of Venice's commercial activities), Castello and Cannaregio (both largely residential), Santa Croce and Dorsoduro. It is said that the curious formal ornament on the prow of a gondola represents the six *sestieri*, with a separate element for the suburb of La Giudecca.

The Venetian dialect has evolved its own idiosyncratic names for localities in addition to Italian words. *Rio* is a narrow canal, while *rio terrà* is one that has been filled in. *Riva* is embankment, *calle* is lane or alley. *Ca'* is short for *casa* (house) and actually refers to a palace. There is only one square or *piazza* in the city, that of St Mark's. All other public open spaces are *campi* (fields) – a reminder of the days when much of the city was green space.

Venice Now

The official population of the city is around 300 000, but one of the problems facing Venice is that fewer and fewer citizens live in the historic centre. In 1950 there were nearly 185 000; today there are barely 80 000, the rest having migrated to Mestre on the mainland. Young married couples, in particular, have decided, reasonably enough, that they prefer to bring up families in comfortable modern apartments on the mainland rather than romantic but damp, dark, frequently cold apartments in the city centre. One of the results of this is that more and more rich 'foreigners' from Milan and the like have set up second homes in the historic areas. Despite all this, and despite

Looking along the lagoon towards St Mark's, with a typically ornate lamp-post in the foreground.

the tremendous pressure of tourism (in the high season there is one visitor for every native inhabitant), the Venetians have, remarkably, retained the Italian gift for actually liking strangers and treating them hospitably.

Venice was linked to the mainland in 1845 when the Austrians built a railway on a causeway. The snarl of motorboats and the chugging of vaporetti are far more common than the song of the gondolier. That apart, the city is much as it was when Bellini or Carpaccio or Canaletto painted it centuries ago, the only major city in the world where the visitor can wander at will, unthreatened and undeafened by traffic – though frequently crushed by fellow tourists. It can be claustrophobic, and it is easy to get lost, for there is no map which details every *calle*. But there's no need to panic: all that is necessary is to keep on walking, and sooner or later you will come to the lagoon or the Grand Canal. It is, after all, an island, and one unique in the world.

Venice in Peril

In November 1966, Italian radio made an extraordinary broadcast: 'High tide in St Mark's Square.' A combination of wind and water had raised the tide nearly seven feet above normal level, so that the Piazza and surrounding buildings were waist-deep in water. What many had feared for nearly a century seemed to be about to happen: Venice was going to disappear into the sea which had given birth to it. It did not happen then, but many believe it is only a question of time before it does.

The problem is twofold: natural and industrial. The entire eastern region is sinking slowly. Datum points in the city show that Venice has sunk nearly seven inches since measurement began in 1908. Natural subsidence has been exaggerated by the vast amount of subterranean water that has been extracted for industrial development on the mainland. In addition, the deep channels dredged to allow large freighters

Combined subsidence and pollution are jeopardizing Venice's future.

The wooden sculpture of Paolo Savelli during resoration.

through the lagoon have altered the primeval pattern of water movements. Pollution, both airborne and waterborne, now attacks the city above and below the waterline.

Looked at objectively, the city's survival is almost miraculous: millions of tons of stone and brick are perched on centuries-old wooden piles driven into soft mud. Essential conservation work is enormous, ranging from restoration of individual sculptures to the creation of a vast new tidal barrier.

The international community has formed a number of emergency committees under the auspices of UNESO to tackle the problem. Foremost among these is *The Venice in Peril Fund* (*see* p.2).

ARCHITECTURE AND ART

The Architecture of Venice

When the Roman emperors abandoned
Rome for Constantinople (Byzantium) they
established their Viceroy (Exarch) in
Ravenna. Venice, emerging from the waves
and seeking an identity, fell under the
influence of that city. The oldest building in
the lagoon, the **Cathedral of Santa Maria
Assunta** on **Torcello**, a settlement founded
in the 7C, clearly shows its ancestry in the
great churches of Ravenna. Byzantine
influence would, in any case, have entered
the city, for trade was with the East and
Eastern ideas came back with the traders.
The great Basilica of St Mark's (the present
building dates from 1063-94) with its domes,
its vast stretches of glittering mosaics and the
solemnity of its interior, is an outstanding
example of original **Byzantine** architecture.

Venice, however, is a northern city, and
inevitably fell under the influence of the
Gothic style, which spread in the 14C from
its origins in France. East met West to
produce the unique hybrid of **Byzantine
Gothic**. The supreme example is the
extension of the **Doges' Palace** (1340-60).
The wealthy merchant princes adopted the
style for their palaces on the Grand Canal, of
which the most outstanding is the **Ca' d'Oro**.

The Venetians continued to use this
distinctive style long after their neighbours
on the mainland had begun to experiment
with the classical forms of the Renaissance.
The **Foscari** and **Giustinian** palaces are in
the same style as the Ca' d'Oro, though built
a century later. The first Renaissance
buildings were the gateway of the **Arsenale**
(1460) and the façade of **St Zachary** (1480).

*The Dome of St
Mark's Basilica
displays the blend
of architectural
styles found in
many Venetian
buildings.*

Outstanding Architects

Most of the architects who later began to put the classical imprint upon the city came from the mainland. The **Lombardi** family came from Padua in the 1460s and built, among much else, the **School of St Mark** (Scuola di San Marco). The Roman **Jacopo Sansovino** arrived in the 1530s and, though primarily a sculptor, designed a remarkable range of buildings, including two of the great palaces, the **Loggetta** at the base of the Campanile and the superb **Libreria Vecchia**.

Andrea Palladio (1508-80) was born in Vicenza and became famous for his villas (later much copied by the English aristocracy), but also designed four of

The Libreria Vecchia, in the Piazzetta San Marco, now houses the Marciana National Library, which has beautiful illuminated manuscripts.

Venice's great churches: **San Giorgio Maggiore**, **St Francis of the Vineyard**, the **Redeemer** and the **Zitelle**. **Baldassarre Longhena** was Venetian by birth, born in 1568. His contribution to his native city, in the Baroque style, included the superb **Santa Maria della Salute** and the **Library** of San Giorgio Maggiore (used as an armoury by the Italian government in the 19C; restored in the 1950s – *see* p.83).

Venetian suspicion of the cult of personality meant that portrait sculpture received little encouragement. **Francesco Foscari**'s decision to place his portrait over the Paper Gate of the Doges' Palace was yet another reason why the Senate suspected his motives. The only reason why **Bartolomeo Colleoni** was eventually allowed his monument was because the Senate was reluctant to lose the vast sum he had bequeathed on condition that the statue was erected. In general, sculpture was regarded as an element of architecture, and many sculptors were also architects.

The Art and Artists of Venice

There could be no clearer indication of the innately conservative character of the Venetians than the fact that the Renaissance came so late to Venice. In nearby Padua, as early as 1313, the great Florentine artist Giotto was making his human figures live and move and express emotions. Over a century later, the figures in the paintings of the Bellini family in Venice were still moving in a statuesque manner.

One of the reasons for Venice's tardiness was its Byzantine tradition. In architecture the Byzantine style was rich and exciting, but applied to painting it was notorious for its

stiffness and formality, and it placed
Venetian art in a kind of straitjacket.
Venetians, too, deeply distrusted the idea of
elevating the individual above society, an
idea that was at the very heart of the
Renaissance.

But when the artists freed themselves
from that straitjacket they did so in a blaze
of colour rarely seen before or since. As one
would expect from the pragmatic, down-to-
earth Venetians, however, colour was firmly
linked to form. **Giovanni Bellini**'s painting
of the Corpus Christi procession in St Mark's
Square is almost photographic in its detail.
Nearly 500 years later, one can identify from
the painting the buildings and details of
buildings around the piazza.

The **Bellinis** – father **Jacopo** (c.1400-71)
and sons **Gentile** (1429-1507) and **Giovanni**
(1430-1516) – were a remarkable dynasty of
artists who acted as a bridge between the
Byzantine Gothic and the new age; their
apprentices included young men who would
in turn emerge as among the greatest artists
of Italy.

It is no easy task to identify authorship of a
Renaissance painting, for the *bottega* ('shop')
system was a kind of mass production. The
master of the bottega would contract to
produce a certain painting. His personal
involvement would depend, to a large
degree, upon the importance of the subject
and the patron. It is fairly certain that
Giovanni Bellini's noble portrait of the Doge
Leonardo Loredan was painted entirely by
Bellini himself. But elsewhere much of the
work would be done by apprentices working
within the grand design laid down by the
master, who would reserve for himself the
more important details.

Veronese's vast work The Feast in the House of Levi *(1573) gives an insight into 16C Venetian life.*

painting of the High Renaissance: **Titian** (*see* next page), **Tintoretto** (1518-94) and **Veronese** (1526-88). Titian's fame was such that he was able to hold his own with the popes and emperors who commissioned him. Nevertheless, even a well-known artist sometimes did have to trim his sails to the prevailing wind, as did Veronese when, in trouble with the Inquisition, he renamed as *The Feast in the House of Levi* an enormous work of 1573, originally called the *Last Supper*.

The artist who, above all, embodies Venetian realism is **Canaletto** (1697-1768). He was a view-painter, a *vedutista*, painting unashamedly for the tourist market with a vivid series of views (*vedute*), frequently using a *camera oscura* for the purpose. He was completely businesslike, entering into a deal with **Joseph Smith**, the British Consul in Venice, to sell his work to the wealthy British aristocrats who flocked into the city. It is for this reason that most of Canaletto's output is in Britain. The Royal Collection alone has more than 50 paintings and 140 drawings.

Titian

It was **Titian** (c.1488-1576), perhaps the greatest of Venetian painters, who laid the foundation of modern art.

He began his apprenticeship at the age of nine or ten and learned his trade in the workshop of the Bellini brothers; he was also a pupil of Giorgione. On Giovanni Bellini's death in 1516, he became official painter to La Serenissima, contracted to paint the portrait of each doge as he took office.

He produced many altarpieces for Venetian churches, as well as portraits of the most powerful figures of the time. One of his most famous is the portrait of the Emperor Charles V, painted in Bologna, and now in Madrid. Later he was to visit Rome where he met Michelangelo.

Another work which is regarded as one of his finest masterpieces is the beautiful *Venus of Urbino* (1538), a reflection of Giorgione's *Sleeping Venus* painted 28 years earlier. His magnificent ceiling painting (1544) for

the church of Santa Maria della Salute can still be seen. Even in his allegorical subjects Titian retains the down-to-earth quality of the Venetian. In his *Bacchanalia*, the central figure holds up against the sky a real Venetian glass, filled, one has the feeling, with wine from the hills around Verona.

Despite being taken up by the great of the time, he maintained his integrity. In his portrait of *Pope Paul III and his two nephews* he shows the effect of absolute power. The foxily senile pope is flanked by his obsequious nephews, the one peering defiantly at the observer, the other humbly genuflecting, smirking at his uncle, clearly prepared to undergo any humiliation so long as he can hold on to the fruits of power. Unsurprisingly, the portrait is unfinished.

Titian returned to Venice in 1550. During this period, he painted many religious and mythical subjects, using the innovative and dramatic effects which were to have a profound influence on the

Titian's Wisdom *can be seen in the Marciana National Library, housed in the Libreria Veccia in the Piazzetta San Marco.*

course of art over the coming centuries. Some of his more notable paintings from this period include the *Annunciation* (1565-6) and *Nymph and Shepherd* (1574). Titian died in Venice on 27 August 1576.

37

THROUGH TRAVELLERS' EYES

The impact of first seeing the city invariably takes visitors by surprise. 'It seemed in the distance like a floating city, its domes, spires, cupolas, and towers, glittering in the sunbeams, looked... like one of those optical illusions,' said Lady Blessington in 1822. **Charles Dickens**, arriving in 1844, wrote to his friend John Forster, 'My dear fellow, nothing in the world that you have ever heard of Venice is equal to the magnificence and stupendous reality. The wildest visions of the Arabian nights are nothing to the piazza of St Mark.'

St Mark's Basilica has been a main attraction for travellers throughout the ages.

Almost all travellers refer to the extraordinary quality of the light. The American novelist **Henry James** said, 'The light here is a mighty magician and with all respect to Titian, Veronese and Tintoretto the greatest artist of them all: a soft iridescence, a lustrous compound of wave and cloud and a hundred nameless local reflections.' In her book *Italian Food*, **Elizabeth David** remarks, 'Of all the spectacular food markets in Italy the one near the Rialto in Venice must be the most remarkable. The light of a Venetian dawn in early summer... is so limpid and so still that it makes every separate vegetable and fruit and fish luminous with a life of its own.'

The paean of praise is not quite universal. The historian **Edward Gibbon** turned aside from his contemplation of Rome to mock Venice: 'Old and in general ill-built houses, ruined pictures and stinking ditches dignified with the pompous denomination of Canals, a fine bridge spoilt by two rows of houses upon it and a large square decorated with the worst Architecture I ever yet saw.' Dickens, after his ecstatic first reaction, was appalled by the prisons, accepting uncritically the legend of their horror: 'Oh God! The nook where the monk came at midnight to confess the political offender: the bench where he was strangled: the deadly little vault where they tied him in a sack and bore him away to sink him where no fisherman dare cast his net.'

Even the insouciant **Casanova** was affected by the legend. Waking in his cell he found himself clutching a cold hand: 'Benumbed with fright I uttered a piercing cry and, dropping the hand I held, I drew back my arm, trembling all over. As I got a little calmer and more capable of reasoning I concluded that a corpse had been placed beside me whilst I was asleep, the body of some strangled wretch to warn me of the fate which is in store for me.' The hand, in fact, was his own: 'deadened by the weight of my body and the hardness of the boards it had lost all sensation'.

Romanticism or Comfort

Henry James, who was there in 1869, has tips for the tourist valuable even today. If you plan to visit the Doges' Palace 'cunningly select your hour – half the enjoyment of Venice is a question of dodging – and enter about one o'clock when the tourists have flocked off to lunch and the echoes of the charming chambers have gone to sleep among the sunbeams.' Wagner listened to two Austrian military bands playing in St Mark's Square 'which offered a truly superb acoustical setting for such music'. However, there was no applause 'for any sign of approbation for an Austrian military band would have been looked upon as treason to the motherland'. The novelist **Stendhal**, although French, agreed. He was there in 1817 and, after enthusing over the beauty of 'this most civilized of cities', ends angrily, 'How I hate Bonaparte for having sacrificed all this to Austria.'

Venice during the period of its decay offered bargains to foreigners, who were able to pick up palaces for a song. **Robert Browning** described how his son bought the Palazzo Rezzonico, 'the finest now obtainable in Venice. He could sell the mere adornments of the building – its statues, pillars, internal decorations and painted cielings [*sic*] (two by Tiepolo) for the full

price of the palazzo itself.'

Romanticism frequently clashed with comfort. **Thomas Moore**, a friend of **Byron**'s, describes the idiosyncratic household the poet had set up in the Palazzo Mocenigo. Moore had wanted to stay in the comfort of a modern hotel. 'As we now turned into the dismal canal and stopped before his damp-looking mansion my predilection for the Gran Bretagna returned in full force and I again ventured to hint that it would save an abundance of trouble to let me proceed thither.' Byron would not hear of it and they entered the palace. 'As I groped my way after him in the dark hall he cried out, "Keep clear of the dog," and before we had proceeded many paces further, "Take care or that monkey will fly at you!"'

The Doges' Palace, with its geometric pink and white marble facades, was the residence of the doges, the seat of government and the law courts.

41

EXPLORING VENICE

MUST SEE

If you have only a limited time in the city, these are the top ten sights you should try to see: **St Mark's Basilica** (Basilica di San Marco), the **Doges' Palace** (Palazzo Ducale), the **Campanile**, the church of **Santa Maria della Salute**, the **Academy** (Accademia), the **Rialto Bridge,** the **School of St Rock** (Scuola di San Rocco), the **Ca' d'Oro** and the islands of **Murano**, **Torcello** and **Burano**.

For a longer stay, four itineraries are suggested.

The magnificent facade of St Mark's Basilica is richly adorned with mosaics, gold statues and, of course, the famous four bronze horses, although those which now stand above the main entrance are copies.

THE HEART OF THE CITY

St Mark's Square

Napoleon described **St Mark's Square** (Piazza San Marco) as 'the finest drawing room in Europe' when he beheld this magnificent square, originally laid out in the 12C on what was an island. The Venetians do, indeed, treat it as a vast open-air salon, including it on the route of the *passeggiata*, the Italian ritual of the evening stroll, and using it as a setting for their major ceremonies. The matched *arcades* which surround it on three sides, giving it that resemblance to an unroofed hall, were built over a period of four centuries. Its world-famous cafés, such as Florian, compete with each other with their resident orchestras – not altogether happily when two or three are playing at the same time.

Campanile

A soaring bell-tower is the dominant characteristic of many an Italian city: it even provides a word for the expression of civic patriotism – *campanilismo*.

Venice's **Campanile** is the oldest and

The Campanile in St Mark's Square is 99m (325ft) high, and affords a fine panorama of Venice.

newest of the city's great structures. The oldest, for it was begun on Roman foundations in the 9C and achieved its final form between 1511 and 1514. The newest, because that tower collapsed at around 10am on 14 July 1902, miraculously without injuring anyone or even damaging the nearby buildings. On the evening of the same day the City Council decreed that it should be rebuilt.

The present vast structure, 99m (325ft) high, was completed in 1912 and is an exact replica. All but one of the five great bells, the ringing of each of which signified a different activity of the day, had been broken and were recast, the gift of Pope Pius X. A spectacular view of the city can be had from the belfry. Sansovino's **Loggetta** at the base of the tower (1537-49) was pieced together again from its fragments.

Almost opposite the Campanile is one of Venice's most popular tourist attractions, the **Clock Tower** (Torre dell'Orologio). Two life-sized figures of Moors strike the hours, as they have done ever since they were cast in 1497. The astronomical clock beneath them dates from the same period.

Piazzetta San Marco

This was the original harbour of the city, with water coming up to the base of the Campanile. The two great columns, one crowned by the Lion of St Mark, the other by St Theodore, were brought from the East

View of the Piazzetta San Marco, showing the column crowned by the Lion of St Mark.

in the 12C. Both statues are made up from fragments of ancient statuary. That of Theodore is a modern copy, the original now being in the Doges' Palace. State executions took place between the columns and Venetians regard it as bad luck to pass between them. Behind the Libreria Vecchia are the **Giardini Reali**, one of the rare green spaces in the city centre.

The famous pair of Moors have been striking the hour on the Clock Tower in St Mark's Square for over 500 years.

The Giardini Reali offer a quiet green oasis – ideal for a rest from sightseeing or a picnic lunch.

St Mark's Basilica

Built between 1063 and 1094, **St Mark's Basilica** (Basilica di San Marco) is the third church on the site, and is the heart and soul of Venice. It has been a cathedral only since 1807. Until then it was, simply, the Doges' Chapel, built less for religious purposes, one feels, than to show the splendour and ruthless power of the republic. The most famous feature, the four life-sized bronze horses on the terrace above the doorways, was looted from Constantinople in 1204.

The four figures known as the Tetrarchs are on the facade of St Mark's Basilica.

Possibly either Greek (4-3C BC) or Roman (4C AD) work, the horses became so much associated with Venice that Napoleon removed them to Paris when he conquered the city; those on the terrace are copies – the originals are housed in the **Marciano Museum** (*see* p.51). On the right-hand corner of the basilica is a strange feature for a Christian building. The four half-life-sized

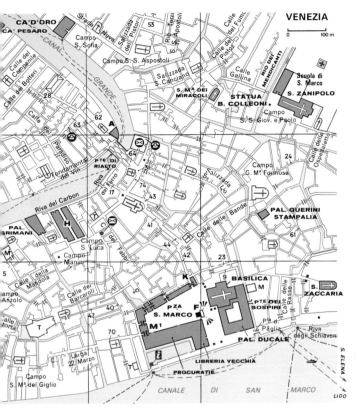

Map of the centre of Venice
K Clock Tower   **M**¹ Correr Museum
F Campanile

4C figures, known as the **Tetrarchs,** in the
reddish-brown stone called porphyry, are
believed to represent the **Emperor
Diocletian** and his three co-rulers – yet
Diocletian was an enemy of Christianity.

Inside and out, the Basilica is one vast picture and sculpture gallery, and the only possible way of absorbing even a fraction of its bewildering richness is through a series of visits.

First examine the **exterior**. The plan of the basilica is that of a Greek cross, with a central dome and a dome over each arm. The five great portals are richly decorated with carvings and mosaics which deserve close inspection. The mosaic above the extreme left-hand door, *Removal of the Body of St Mark* (1260-70), shows the oldest representation of the church, with the bronze horses already in position. The carvings of the under-arch of the main, central, door represent Venetian trades: the bronze door with the lion's head is 11C Byzantine.

The main doorway leads into the narthex or entrance hall, which runs round three

The mosaic over one of the basilica portals depicts the Removal of the Body of St Mark.

sides of the western arm. The tomb on the right of the doorway is probably the oldest in Venice, being that of the Doge Falier Vitale (d.1096). The intarsia floor is of the 11C-12C. The white lozenge set in a slab of reddish stone marks the spot where the Emperor Barbarossa knelt before Pope Alexander II in 1177. Mosaics in the domes are based on Old Testament themes. Doors lead up to the **Marciano Museum** (Museo Marciano) where the original bronze horses are housed, and to the terrace with its superb view of the Square.

Close-up detail of one of the mosaics on the facade of St Mark's Basilica.

The Lion of St Mark

Scattered throughout Venice, and placed on columns or over portals in every city conquered by Venice on the mainland or in the Eastern Mediterranean, you will find the figure of a winged lion with its paw on an open book. The words *Pax tibi Marce* *evangelista meum* can be read on the book. A winged lion is the emblem of Mark the Evangelist, whose association with the city is both macabre and an ingenious piece of propaganda. The Venetians already had a patron saint, an obscure easterner called

PA X VAN
TIBI GELI
MAR STA
CE E MEVS

Theodore who, with his crocodile, is still to be seen on one of the columns in the Piazzetta. But as the city grew, a grander figure was needed.

A timely prophecy was discovered. It was said that when St Mark was travelling by ship to Rome he docked at the Rialto, and an angel appeared to him in a dream, saying *Pax tibi Marce, evangelista meum. Hic requiescet corpus tuum* ('Peace to thee, Mark, my evangelist. Here your body shall rest').

Mark in fact died and was buried in Alexandria in Egypt. About the year 830 two Venetian merchants in Alexandria plundered his tomb and stole the body. In order to smuggle it past the customs post they packed lumps of pork around it, from which the devout Muslims shrank, crying '*Kanzir, kanzir*' ('pig, pig').

The scene is depicted in detail among the mosaics of St Mark's, and although it is, as with all medieval legends, full of holes, not only Venice but the entire Christian world accepted that the corpse in the splendid new basilica was indeed that of the writer of the Second Gospel.

A city possessing the relics of even an ordinary saint enjoyed prestige. Venice's possession of the entire body of one of the Disciples placed it second only to Rome, with its body of St Peter himself.

The winged Lion of St Mark, by Vittore Carpaccio.

The level of lighting of the **interior** of St Mark's Basilica varies greatly according to the time of year and day: sometimes shadowy, sometimes a blaze of gold and coloured mosaic. It is illuminated from 11.30am-12.30pm weekdays, on Saturday afternoons, and all day on Sundays and holidays. Just about every inch of the walls is covered with mosaic on a background of gold leaf, to a total of 4 000sq m (4780sq yd), mostly created between the 11C and 13C. A booklet on sale in the church identifies most of them. Running round the interior is a narrow gallery which provides both a general view and an opportunity to study the mosaics at close quarters.

The basilica also contains some of the world's most precious marble. Look for the remarkable 'parrot' sequence: a fault in a

Detail of the richly coloured mosaic floor of St Mark's Basilica.

block of marble has taken the shape of a parrot and the block has been sliced into panels. The undulating pavement with its intricate designs, dates from the 12C-13C. Separating the sanctuary from the nave is the *iconostasis* or rood screen, made of reddish marble from Verona and decorated with geometric forms of coloured marbles. The body of St Mark is in a **sarcophagus** beneath the high altar.

Behind the altar is one of the richest objects in this treasure house, the **Golden Screen** (*Pala D'Oro*), a blaze of precious stones, metals and enamel, crammed with detail. Its construction spanned some 400 years, for it was originally commissioned in Constantinople in 976 by Doge **Pietro Orseolo.** Enamels looted from Constantinople were added after 1204 and further additions completed the screen in 1345. The **treasury**, leading off the south transept, contains one of the richest collections of Byzantine artwork, much of it stolen from Constantinople after its sacking in 1204. The baptistery contains what John Ruskin called 'the best existing example of Venetian monumental sculpture' – the tomb of Doge **Andrea Dandolo** (d.1354).

Doges' Palace

Nothing better illustrates the immense self-confidence of the Venetians than the fact that the **Doges' Palace** (Palazzo Ducale) is indeed a palace, not a castle. In all other Italian cities, even Rome, the medieval or Renaissance seat of government is heavily fortified – as much against the citizens as against outside enemies. The Venetians were confident that no enemy could penetrate their lagoon and threaten their Great

Council and no citizen would dream of opposing it. The Doges' Palace is probably the world's best secular example of that Gothic style usually reserved for churches.

Like its immediate neighbour the basilica, the Doges' Palace is the third building on the site. The first building, erected in the turbulence of the 9C, was actually a fortified castle complete with drawbridge. This, and its successor, were destroyed by fire. The purpose of the present building, commenced in 1345, was to provide a worthy setting for the supreme governing body not only of the city but of the seaborne empire Venice had acquired. It was the ceremonial seat of the doges, but also of the various interlocking councils which constituted the

The magnificent Doges' Palace symbolized Venice's power and glory.

government as well as the law courts – and it contained the prison. Two more great fires, in 1574 and 1577, meant that most of the present-day interior decoration is post-16C.

The palace is double-fronted, one façade facing the lagoon, the other the Piazzetta. Entrance is on the Piazzetta side through

The Porta della Carta was built in 1442 in the Flamboyant-Gothic style.

the richly decorated **Paper Gate** (Porta della Carta), so called because decrees were posted there. The group above the door, showing Doge Foscari (1423-57) kneeling before the Lion of St Mark, is a 19C copy placed there in 1885. The original was destroyed by Napoleon's men. The Gate leads through the **Foscari** porch and arch, with its cluster of statues, into the vast courtyard, flanked on the left by the bulk of the basilica. Immediately ahead is the **Giants' Staircase** (Scala dei Giganti), the ceremonial entrance into the palace guarded by **Sansovino**'s colossal statues of Mercury and Neptune (1566).

As with all Italian palaces, the ground floor was used for various everyday functions. The first floor contained the doge's apartments. The palace is a maze of rooms, most of them officially open to the public but frequently closed for restoration. All are identified by signs. The most magnificent chamber is the **College Hall** (Sala del Collegio) on the top floor. Beneath a superb gilded ceiling with paintings by **Veronese**, the doge and his councillors received foreign embassies or listened to the reports of Venetian ambassadors returned from foreign parts.

Just as magnificent is the **Waiting Room** (Anticollegio), designed by **Palladio**, where those summoned to the presence awaited their turn. On the same floor is the **Meeting Room** of the sinister **Council of Ten** (Consiglio dei Dieci): founded in 1310 after the uncovering of a conspiracy, this acted as a committee of safety along the lines of the Gestapo or KGB. In an antechamber called the **Compass Room** (Sala della Bussola) is the infamous Lion's Mouth where secret

Giovanni-Battista Tiepolo's portrayal of Neptune offering gifts to Venice forms part of a ceiling fresco in the Doges' Palace.

denunciations were posted. The doge's private residence on the first floor contains paintings which survived the fire, among them the *Lion of St Mark* by **Carpaccio**.

Overlooking the lagoon on the same floor is the immense **Great Council Chamber** (Sala del Maggior Consiglio), built to hold all the 2,500 patricians of the Great Council entitled to ratify all laws and elect the government. The fire of 1577 destroyed a treasury of Renaissance paintings but the Hall was restored with even greater splendour, including the work of such artists as **Tintoretto**, **Veronese**, **Palma** and their followers and pupils. The vast gold ceiling has Veronese's *Apotheosis of Venice* and it is impossible to miss Tintoretto's immense *Paradiso*, with its hundreds of figures. Tintoretto was also commissioned to paint the frieze showing the first 76 doges which runs round three sides of the room. One of the portraits carries the ominous warning that even a doge's power is limited. The portrait of Marin Faliero is veiled in black: he was beheaded for conspiracy in 1355.

THE GRAND CANAL

Sweeping through the heart of the city in the shape of an 'S' written backwards, some 4km (2½ miles) long, the Grand Canal is Venice's 'High Street'. Nobles vied with each other to build ever more splendid palaces along it; foreigners built their depots upon it; fishermen and farmers displayed their wares in markets beside it.

Most of the palaces bear family names, and nothing more dramatically illustrates the sheer wealth of Venice in its heyday than the homes of these merchant princes. Although individualistic, they share common characteristics. None has the defensive features of the fortress-like palaces on the mainland. They have a landward entrance as well as an entrance on the Canal itself, where a landing stage has *pali* or poles to secure the family gondolas. An entrance hall runs through the whole building, but the ground floor is mostly storage space or is sometimes let out as shops. The main living area is the splendid and aptly named *piano nobile* (noble floor) on the first floor.

The lovely Church of Santa Maria della Salute was built by Longhena at the entrance of the Grand Canal in the 17C.

A ride in a vaporetto is an excellent way to explore the Grand Canal.

The western side of the Canal is known as **Dorsoduro** ('hard back'), for its ground is relatively hard. The eastern side is **Rialto** (*riv' alto*, 'high embankment'). The frequent, cheap water-buses (*vaporetti*) which travel along it provide an excellent viewing platform as they zigzag between the banks.

The journey from St Mark's Square to the railway station takes about 40 minutes and is an admirable way to gain an overall picture of the city. The individual buildings can then be visited later on foot. The list below comprises only the major buildings which can be seen from the Grand Canal when travelling up from St Mark's Basin. Included is a selection of the canals to provide orientation.

L = left bank; R = right bank.

L **Customs Point** (Punta della Dogana) is where St Mark's Basin, the Grand Canal and the Canale della Giudecca meet, and was the place where incoming vessels deposited their cargoes for taxing. The tower-shaped building on the very point was built in 1677. It is surmounted by the golden Ball of Fortune, held aloft by two Atlases.

L **Santa Maria della Salute** after the Campanile and St Mark's, this great church on its prominent site is probably the most photographed building in the city. The church was dedicated to Our Lady 'of Salvation' in thanksgiving for the ending of a disastrous plague which carried off a third of the population in 1630.

The architect was the 26-year-old **Baldassarre Longhena**, who adopted an entirely new form, heavy with symbolism: as he put it, 'a virgin work... strange, worthy and beautiful, in shape of a round

"machine" such as had never before been seen or invented'. Built on a raised platform which is supported by more than a million close-packed wooden piles, it is in the form of an octagon, symbolizing Mary's star, with a single immense cupola that is her crown.

The interior is a treasure-house of statuary and paintings, among them one of **Titian**'s earliest works, portraying four saints (1511),

The Grand Canal, complete with colourful gondolas, is an unforgettable sight. The Customs Point, with its Golden Ball of Fortune, is on the left.

in the Sacristy, and the *Marriage Feast at Cana* by **Tintoretto** (1561), one of his most important works.

ʟ Campo della Salute.

ʀ Rio della Luna.

ʀ The **Port Authority** (*Capitaneria di Porto*) was built in the Lombardic style at the end of the 15C.

ʀ Calle del Ridotto.

ʀ The **Ca' Giustinian** was built c.1474 for the powerful family of the Giustiniani. Today it houses municipal offices and the **Biennial Art Exhibition**.

The Palazzetto Contarini-Fasan is said to have been the home of Desdemona, Othello's wife.

R Rio di san Moisè.

L Rio della Salute.

R The **Palazzetto Contarini-Fasan** was built c.1475, and is an excellent example of Venetian Gothic. It is the legendary home of **Desdemona**, Othello's ill-fated wife.

R Rio delle Ostreghe.

R **Palazzo Gritti** is Venetian Gothic, of the early 15C. The façade was originally decorated by **Giorgione**. It is now an hotel – **Hemingway** enjoyed many a sundowner on the balcony.

L **Palazzo Dario** is famous for the intricate

The 20C writer Henri de Régnier lived in the Palazzo Dario.

decorations and brightly coloured marbles of its façade. It was built about 1487 for **Giovanni Dario**, the republic's representative in Constantinople.

L Campo and Rio San Vio.

L Palazzo Venier dei Leoni, a colossal unfinished palace, begun 1749, is now the home of the **Guggenheim Collection** (*see* p.90). According to tradition, the Venier family kept a lion in the garden behind, hence its name.

L Palazzo Loredan was built in the mid-16C. At the turn of the 19-20C it was the home of **Don Carlos di Borbone,** Pretender to the Spanish throne.

R Rio di San Maurizio.

R The name of the **Palazzo Corner della Ca' Grande** (Ca' Grande = big house) refers to its immense size. It was begun in 1532 to a design by **Sansovino**; its construction took over 30 years. The home of the Corner, one

The Palazzo Corner della Ca' Grande dwarfs the neighbouring buildings.

The Palazzo Contarini dal Zaffo is built in fine Renaissance style.

of the richest of Venetian families, its interior was sumptuous. It is now the seat of the Prefecture.

L The perfect Renaissance façade of the **Palazzo Contarini dal Zaffo** was designed towards the end of the 15C. Inside are friezes by **Domenico Tiepolo** (1696-1770). The splendid decorated ceiling was looted by the Germans in World War II and its return is still a subject of controversy.
R Rio del Santissimo.

The **Palazzi Barbaro** are twin palaces built for the same family. The left-hand palace is 15C, the right-hand one 17C. Among the many distinguished foreigners who lodged

The Palazzi Barbaro have offered hospitality to many famous visitors in their time, including the novelist Henry James.

in the older palace was the novelist **Henry James**: 'A bed was put up for me in this divine old library where I am fain to pass the live-long day.'

R **Palazzo Franchetti** is of the 15C. Note its central windows, which were inspired by the Doges' Palace.

Apart from the Rialto and the modern railway bridge, the **Bridge of the Academy** (Ponte dell'Accademia) is the only bridge across the Grand Canal. The original bridge, built by the Austrians in 1854, was of iron. It was too low to allow the passage of vaporetti and was replaced by a 'temporary' wooden bridge in 1932. This was replaced in 1985 by the replica you see today.

R **Palazzo Giustiniani-Lolin** was begun in 1623; it is a youthful work by **Longhena**, before he became famous.

L **The Academy of Fine Arts** (Gallerie

dell'Accademia) was built in 1760; it houses one of Europe's most important collections of paintings (*see* p.89).

L Palazzo Loredan degli Ambasciatori was built in the 15C in the Gothic style. In the 18C it was the home of the Austrian ambassadors to the Republic.

L Palazzo Rezzonico was begun by **Longhena** c.1650, and completed in 1745. The Grand Staircase is one of the most splendid in the city. The son of the poet **Robert Browning** married an American heiress and bought the palace in 1888. Browning himself lived in it, and died there in 1889. Today the palace houses the **Venice in the 18C Museum**.

L Calle Bernardo.

L Ca' Foscari was where Doge **Francesco Foscari** died a week after being forced out of office in 1457 (*see* p.13-14). Foscari

View along the Grand Canal from the Ponte dell'Accademia.

demolished a previous palace on the site and built the present majestic edifice for himself, giving the patricians further grounds to suspect him of self-aggrandisement. **Henri III** of France stayed in the palace during a grand visit to Venice in 1572.

R One of the few palaces to be built by non-Venetians, the **Palazzo Grassi** was the home of the Bolognese family of Grassi. It was built around 1718 when they were admitted into the ranks of the Venetian aristocracy, and is in the classic 18C style. Today it is a major exhibition and conference centre.

L **Veronese** painted his vast picture *The Family of Darius before Alexander* for the equally vast and grand reception hall of the **Palazzo Pisani Moretta**. It is now in London's National Gallery, but the works of Tiepolo and Piazzetta are still *in situ*.

L Calle dell Traghetto di San Benedetto.

R The four great palaces side by side, the

The Ca' Foscari was the residence and final refuge of Doge Foscari.

Case dei Mocenigo, belonged to one family, the Mocenigo. They range in date from the 15C to the 17C. **Byron** lived in the central, double one with lions' heads on the façade.

R **Palazzo Contarini dei Cavalli** was built in the Gothic style c.1445. It takes its name from the two horses that are part of the coat-of-arms on the façade.

R Rio San Luca.

R Built to overawe, the vast Renaissance **Palazzo Grimani** (c.1550) is the work of the Veronese architect **Michele Sanmicheli**. It is now the Court of Appeal.

The graceful Rialto Bridge was originally designed to allow ships to sail through.

EXPLORING VENICE

The **Rialto Bridge** (Ponte di Rialto) dates from the 16C. Curiously, the Venetians, so proud of the appearance of their city, were content to have a series of 'temporary' wooden bridges at this busy spot for over 300 years.

The first was built c.1250. At least two of its successors collapsed before it was decided, in 1524, to build a permanent bridge in stone. Michelangelo was among those who submitted designs, but the commission was given to a relative unknown, **Antonio da Ponte**. After years of wrangling, work commenced in 1588 and was completed in 1592.

The bridge is lined on either side with shops and provides a world-famous view of the Grand Canal. **Carpaccio**'s painting *Miracle of the True Cross* (c.1500) shows that the previous wooden bridge had a drawbridge in the middle to allow the passage of ships.

The sharp bend of the Canal beyond the bridge is known as the **Volta del Canale.**
R Foreign merchants had their own organizations in the city. The **Fondaco dei Tedeschi** was the headquarters of the Germans, combining storage and living areas. It was built about 1508 and today serves as the General Post Office.

R **Ca' da Mosto**, dating from the 13C in a characteristic Venetian-Byzantine design, has had a varied history. It was the home of the seafaring Da Mosto family. From the 15C to the 18C it became famous as the *Albergo del Leon Bianco* (White Lion Inn).

L **Fish market** (Pescheria): there has been a fish market on this site for centuries, but the present elegant building, based on a 15C design, was erected in 1907.

The most elegant Ca' d'Oro, built in Gothic style, is one of the most famous frontages on the Grand Canal.

R The most famous palace on the Canal is the **Ca' d'Oro**. There is uncertainty about the origins of its name. One suggestion is that its name 'Golden House' is derived from the rich gilding which once adorned the façade. An alternative suggestion is that its name refers to the family Doro which once lived there. Built between 1421 and 1440, it is, in fact, unfinished, for it was intended to have two flanking wings. It has a particularly fine courtyard, with the characteristic Venetian *pozzo* (well). The building now houses the Franchetti Gallery (*see* p.89-90).

R Rio della Pergola.

R The **Fondaco dei Turchi** was the headquarters of the Turkish merchants from 1621 to 1838; the original building dates back to the 13C. It belonged to the Dukes of Ferrara and the interior was so splendid that the Senate frequently borrowed it for State occasions. It was almost entirely rebuilt in the 19C, using materials from the first building. Today, it houses the **Natural History Museum** (Museo di Storia Naturale).

R **Palazzo Vendramin-Calergi** was begun about 1500; it is one of the first major buildings in the city to be designed in the classical Renaissance manner. The composer **Richard Wagner** lived in this house from September 1882 and died here in February 1883. He chose it because it had a heating system, a rarity at the time, when many of the buildings in Venice were notoriously damp.

L The **railway bridge** was built in 1934 to replace the bridge put up by the Austrians in 1858. The railway station, opened in 1861, was rebuilt in 1955.

BEYOND THE CITY CENTRE

The city centre is fascinating, but sooner or later the visitor will find the need to escape the narrow alleys. While remaining in the historic area, this itinerary will take you along the lagoon to Venice's only large **Public Gardens** (Giardini Pubblici) – ironically, created at the behest of Napoleon. Curving to the east, the walk takes in a gradually widening panorama.

The Bridge of Sighs

Leave St Mark's Square by the Piazzetta, passing the **Bridge of Sighs** (Ponte dei Sospiri) on the left. Built in 1600, the bridge connects the Doges' Palace with the **New**

Gondolas passing beneath the famous Bridge of Sighs, connecting the Doges' Palace with the New Prison.

Prison (Prigioni Nuove). Prisoners walking from one to the other presumably sighed as they took their last look at the outside world through the barred windows. It was **Byron** who, in *Childe Harold's Pilgrimage*, made the bridge famous for English-speaking visitors ('I stood in Venice on the Bridge of Sighs/A palace and a prison on each hand'). Conditions in Venetian prisons were exaggerated by Venice's enemies, paarticularly the 18C French: life was no worse than in other prisons of the period.

Riva degli Schiavoni
Ahead lies the long and handsome expanse of the **Riva degli Schiavoni.** The quay takes its name from the Dalmatian sailors

There are plentiful opportunities to sit and take in the views over a drink at a café on the Riva degli Schiavoni.

The Gothic-style façade of the Hotel Danieli, haunt of the rich and famous, fronts the Canal di San Marco.

(Slavonians) who anchored their trading vessels here. Large vessels still tie up at it, enabling tourists to step off the ship straight into the 'drawing room' of Venice. From the Riva the panorama of the city begins to open out. Just before the little bridge there is a combined jewel and eyesore, the **Hotel Danieli**. The hotel was originally the Palazzo Dandolo, built in 15C Gothic style, and much of its splendid interior has been preserved, including 18C frescoes. It was turned into an hotel in 1822. Its guests have included **George Sand** and **Charles Dickens**, and it is still the haunt of international celebrities with deep purses. The annexe, built in 1948, has been bitterly criticized for its jarring appearance.

Church of St Zachary (San Zaccaria)
The **Church of St Zachary** was dedicated to the father of John the Baptist (his body is

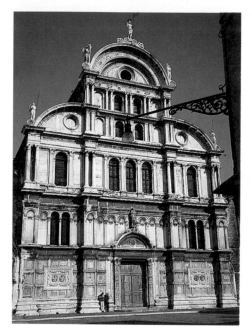

The Church of St Zachary, built in a mixture of styles, houses some notable works of art.

reputed to be found in the crypt). The building of this ancient church covers some 600 years, from the 9C when it was founded by the Byzantine **Emperor Leo X** to the 15C when it was substantially rebuilt. It is an amalgam of Byzantine, Gothic and Renaissance styles, and includes the original 9C crypt, the burial place of the first doges, the unique Byzantine ambulatory built for ceremonial processions and the Renaissance façade by **Antonio Gambello** (1480-1500). Outstanding among the many paintings is **Giovanni Bellini's** *Virgin and Child*, painted in his maturity (1506). It came into French hands in 1797, but was returned in 1818.

Inland from the Riva

It will be necessary to walk inland from the Riva to see the church of **St Francis of the Vineyard** (San Francesco della Vigna). The present church, designed by Sansovino, was built between 1534 and 1572. The facade is by Palladio, and inside is **Giovanni Bellini**'s painting of the *Virgin and Child*. The foundation stone was laid by one of the great doges, **Andrea Gritti**, who is buried in the church.

A school (*scuola*) was a meeting place for people of a particular craft or profession. The **School of St George of the Dalmatians** (Scuola di San Giorgio degli Schiavoni) was the headquarters of the Dalmatian merchants of Venice and has a superb series of frescoes by **Carpaccio** (1502-8).

The School of St George of the Dalmatians served people from Dalmatia, notably seamen, who lived in Venice.

The Arsenal (Arsenale)

The main docks of the **Arsenal** open on to
the distant northern shore (*see* p.18). It was
an indication of its importance to Venice
that the great **gateway**, built in 1460, is the
first major Renaissance structure in the city.
The **Lion of St Mark** above it holds a closed,
not open, book, for it was felt inappropriate
that the words *Pax Tibi* ('Peace be unto
thee'), which can usually be read on the
book, should be seen on a building devoted
to war.

The four lions that guard the gate are war
booty from the Eastern Mediterranean. The

*The winged lion
proudly guards the
entrance to the
Arsenal.*

The Public Gardens (Giardini Pubblici) are one of the few green places in Venice.

large upright lion and its recumbent partner come from the Piraeus, and were brought here by Doge **Francesco Morosini** in 1687. The scratchmarks on the large lion are runes, carved by members of the Varangian Guard of Norsemen, who had subdued the Piraeus for Byzantium in 1040. The towers on either side of the canal date to 1574.

Other sights

Isola di San Pietro, now a lonely and unfashionable island, was the first part of Venice to be colonized. The church of St Peter (San Pietro) was originally the cathedral of Venice, but over the centuries lost ground to the basilica of St Mark, to which the bishopric was moved in 1807. The present church, completed in 1596, was designed by **Palladio.**

The **Isola di Sant'Elena**, the easternmost point of the city, has lovely **Public Gardens** (Giardini Pubblici). The centre section of the three gardens forms the venue for the **Biennale Festival** (*see* p.97). Beyond lies the little 15C church of **St Helen** (Sant'Elena).

THE ISLANDS OF THE LAGOON

San Giorgio Maggiore

Immediately opposite the Piazzetta and a few hundred yards away across the lagoon is what appears to be a mirror-image of the great Campanile. It is the campanile of the church and monastery of **San Giorgio Maggiore**. The island on which it stands has had a decidedly mixed history. Founded in the 10C, the monastery was patronized by the great and powerful. The fabulously rich Florentine banker **Cosimo de' Medici**

Water taxis speed past the island of San Giorgio Maggiore.

enjoyed a comfortable exile there in the 1430s and repaid it by lending the monks his personal architect, **Michelozzo**. Others followed suit and by the end of the 18C San Giorgio Maggiore was a harmonious work of art, a complex of gardens and buildings created by Italy's leading architects and artists.

In 1803, the occupying French turned the monastery into a barracks. Their decision was logical, if deplorable, for the island had strategic importance, but, astonishingly, the Italian government continued the vandalization by establishing an artillery headquarters in the monastery in 1851. In 1951, however, the wealthy industrialist and philanthropist **Count Vittorio Cini** undertook to restore the complex in memory of his son, who had been killed in an air crash. The monks have returned and the rest of the island is occupied by the **Fondazione Cini**, a cultural organization. The church, built between 1565 and 1610, is by **Palladio**, who also designed one of the two beautiful cloisters, and the interior has works by **Tintoretto** and his school.

La Giudecca

Separated from the main body of the city by the deep Giudecca Canal, this long, narrow group of eight connected islands acted as a kind of suburb. Until relatively recently it was famous for the private gardens of the wealthy residents (the quaintly named Garden of Eden, named after its English owner, still survives), and there are pleasant quiet corners. There has been a considerable amount of recent development, including factories, and it is one of the few areas of historic Venice where

modern apartments have been built. The great **Church of the Redeeme**r (Redentore) was designed by **Palladio** in 1577 to mark the end of a plague (this is still celebrated as a festival, *see* p.97). By contrast is the engaging little church, the **Zitelle,** also the work of **Palladio**. The attached convent was a home for poor girls, who produced the exquisite *punto in aria* lace.

Zitelle Church, on the island of La Giudecca.

Murano

This is virtually a miniature Venice, complete with its own Grand Canal. It had its own system of government, all but independent of the mother city, and its own mint. In the 16C it was a favoured resort of wealthy Venetians who wanted green fields and fresh air near their homes. There was a population of 30 000 and no fewer than 17 churches. Today the population has dwindled to a handful and there are only two churches, but one of them, dedicated to **Santi Maria e Donato**, is worth the journey. Although founded in the 7C, it was substantially rebuilt in the 12C and is an almost unspoiled example of Venetian Byzantine architecture. Its mosaic floor, created around 1141, is even more splendid than St Mark's.

The island's chief glory, and the reason for its relative independence, is its world-famous glass industry, removed from Venice proper in 1291 because of the danger of fire. The glass-makers enjoyed many privileges but were forbidden to leave Venice in case they took their vital trade secrets with them. There is an important **Glass Museum** (Museo di arte vetraria) housed in a 16C palace. Its 4 000-odd exhibits include Roman, Egyptian and Phoenician work.

The charming church of Santi Maria e Donato, on Murano, is well worth a visit.

These brightly painted houses are characteristic of Burano.

Burano

This lively little island, with its brilliantly painted houses, has come back to life after many years in the industrial doldrums. Fishing is its major industry but its lace-making – a craft for which it was famous for centuries – has been revived and contributes substantially to its prosperity.

Burano is famous for the quality of its hand-made lace.

Torcello

The island was the first to be occupied by the refugees of the 7C and even had its own bishopric, established in 638. Its cathedral, begun in 639 and rebuilt in 1008, is the oldest building on all the islands of the lagoon. The façade is 9C but most of the present structure was built in the early 11C. The interior has all the solemnity and austerity of the Byzantine tradition, and is built in a delicate green-grey marble which contrasts with the rich marble mosaics. The most important mosaic is the *Final Judgement*, on the west wall. The dome of the apse has a magnificent 12C mosaic of the Madonna and Child. Other mosaics were inspired by the 6C examples in Ravenna.

The Lido

One of the two vital seaward defences of the city has now become its playground. Until late in the 19C it consisted mostly of open country, but it has now been heavily developed for the tourist trade. Most of the beaches are private, but there are two open to the public.

Pellestrina

This is worth visiting if only to see the vast sea-walls (*murazzi*). Completed in 1751, they were one of the very last works of the free Republic. Despite their massiveness, they were badly breached in the great flood of November 1966. There is little else of historic interest, but the island, with its little fishing villages, provides a delightful break from the bustle of the city.

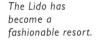

The Lido has become a fashionable resort.

MUSEUMS AND GALLERIES

The following is only a selection of the 30 or so museums and galleries in Venice, indicating those which should not be missed if time permits. Besides these, it is probably safe to say that every public building, and certainly every important church, in Venice has at least one major work by a major artist and a treasury of work by other artists who would be regarded as outstanding in any other country but Italy. Although paintings in churches are overtly religious, the Venetians delighted in background detail. When visiting churches, be well supplied with lire coins. Most churches now have coin-operated lighting systems which supply essential illumination for brief periods.

Academy of Fine Arts
(Gallerie dell'Accademia)
Officially attached to the School of Art, this was founded by **Eugénie Napoleon** in 1807; most of its exhibits were taken from churches and monasteries suppressed by Napoleon and so form a collection of Italian art from the earliest times to the 18C, with emphasis on Venetian painting. Room V is entirely devoted to the works of **Giovanni Bellini** and perhaps the finest work of his follower, **Giorgione**, *The Tempest* (*see* p.34). In Room X is **Paolo Veronese's** vast painting, *The Feast in the House of Levi* (*see* p.35).

Franchetti Gallery
Baron Giorgio Franchetti donated Ca' d'Oro and its contents to the city in 1916. He had restored it as far as possible to its original appearance (even re-acquiring the well-head and external staircase, which had been sold off), and the exhibits are

arranged to look like an aristocratic Venetian home of the 15C rather than a museum. The first floor has as its major feature the famous *St Sebastian* by **Andrea Mantegna** (c.1500).

Guggenheim Collection
This collection is housed in the unfinished Palazzo Venier dei Leoni, which the American art collector **Peggy Guggenheim**

Vittore Carpaccio's Arrival of St Ursula during the Siege of Cologne, 1490-94, is in the Academy of Fine Arts.

The Palazzo Venier dei Leoni houses the famous Guggenheim Collection.

occupied from 1949 to her death in 1970. It is now administered by a trust. The collection concentrates on modern art, including work by **Chagall**, **Giacometti**, **Klee** and **Picasso**.

Venice in the 18C Museum
(Museo del Settecento Veneziano)

Situated in the vast Ca' Rezzonico, the museum (currently being restored) is planned to show Venetian social life in the ostentatiously opulent 18C. On the *piano nobile* is the enormous **ballroom** with a series of remarkable architectural perspectives, and the **Throne Room** with its Rococo ceiling by **Tiepolo** (1696-1770), the last of the great Venetian decorators. The second floor has the more intimate family apartments, including the room in which **Robert Browning** died.

91

Libreria Vecchia

Begun in 1540 by **Jacopo Sansovino**, it
earned an accolade from no less a person
than Palladio as 'the richest and most
decorated building ever perhaps created
from ancient times until today'. It is also
known as the **Sansovinian Library**. A grand
staircase leads up to the showpiece, the great
Golden Hall (Sala Dorata) with paintings by
Veronese and **Tintoretto**. On display are
treasures from the Libreria Vecchia (Old
Library), including Byzantine miniatures
and Renaissance illuminated books.
(Entrance free but by request.)

Correr Museum

This vast and ever-growing museum
illustrates Venice's history. It is housed in the
Ala Napoleonica (Napoleonic Wing), which
forms one side of St Mark's Square. There is
an excellent art gallery and a section
illustrating Venice's struggle against Austria.

Museum of Naval History
(Museo Storico Navale)

Appropriately housed near the Arsenal, the
museum tells the story of Venice's naval
history with models of the fighting galleys.
An outstanding exhibit is a large-scale model
of the last **Bucintoro**, the great state barge.

Great School of St Rock
(Scuola Grande di San Rocco)

The Scuola was the headquarters of a
confraternity dedicated to the relief of the
sick, with St Rock as its patron. Commenced
in 1515, the building was completed in 1560
and in 1564 **Tintoretto** began a series of
commissions for it which were to occupy
him for 24 years. One of the greatest of

Venetian artists, he was also one of the least popular, disliked for his avarice and his habit of filching commissions from fellow artists. Nevertheless, John Ruskin compared his work in the Scuola with Michelangelo's in the Sistine Chapel. The theme is religious painting on a grand scale: the *Crucifixion* occupies one entire wall. *Christ before Pilate* is regarded as one of his greatest works.

Beyond the horse statue, the two Moors can just be seen striking the hour on the top of the Clock Tower, St Mark's Square.

ENJOYING YOUR VISIT

The Playground of Europe

It is by a quirk of history that Venice, the home of a somewhat dour people compared with their volatile mainland cousins, should have become notorious for its luxury and depravity in the 17C and 18C. The Venetian courtesan was already an established figure. **Thomas Coryat**, who walked to Venice from England in 1608, met one of these splendid creatures and was so agog with the experience that he included in his book a picture of himself saluting her.

The courtesan was by no means a common prostitute but had a wide range of social skills, not unlike the Japanese geisha. She could sing, accompanying herself on the lute. She could discourse intelligently on cultural subjects. She could preside gracefully at a banquet. The rich and powerful flocked eagerly to the salons of the more famous ones. But she was also well aware of her value. If a client made off without paying, Coryat said, 'She will either cause thy throate to be cut by her ruffiano or procure thee to be arrested and clapped into prison.'

Gambling was introduced in the 18C by the aristocratic Dandolo family, who set aside part of their palace for the purpose. In return for permission to do this, the government took a share in the profits. And the profits were large, for the Dandolo casino became famous all over Europe. (Gambling in the city is still run by the local authority.) But over and above the attractions of the courtesans and gambling it was the Venetian Carnival which attracted visitors from all over the world.

The elaborate masks are a central part of the Carnival.

Carnival

There is an irony in the fact that the word *Carnevale* means 'farewell to flesh' – in other words, preparation for the Lenten fast – for the Venetian Carnival became a byword for its sensuousness. Officially it ran from Boxing Day to Shrove Tuesday, but it proved such a money-spinner that gradually it occupied the better part of the year. Masks were *de rigueur*, lending the frisson of anonymity which encouraged outrageous behaviour. A shocked Englishman, Francis

Misson, witnessed the Carnival of 1688: 'They are not satisfied with the ordinary Libertinism... the whole city is disguised. Vice and Vertue are never so well counterfeited. The place of St Mark is fill'd with a Thousand sorts of Jack Puddings, Strangers and Courtesans come in Shoals from all parts of Europe.' The Earl of Perth was equally shocked around 1790: 'We saw what in Scotland would be thought downright madness: everybody is in a mask, a thing of taffeta is put on the head which covers one's face to the nose.'

The Carnival was revived in the 1970s for the same reason as the Wedding with the Sea: it brings in tourist cash. But the Venetians themselves take part in it, and while it lacks the licence of the 18C, it is still an exciting time, given additional impetus by being limited to ten days before Lent. As in the 17C, St Mark's Square is the main venue. Sober businessmen can be seen wearing the traditional taffeta mask, while at the other extreme, adults and children alike wear elaborate fancy dress.

Other Festivals

Apart from the Carnival and the **Wedding of the Sea** (*see* p.20), Venice has five other major festivals unique to the city.
The 'Long Row' (Vogalonga) takes place on Ascension Day (the same day as the Wedding and associated with it). It is a 40km (25miles) boat-race around the lagoon, finishing up in St Mark's Basin. Hundreds take part, including elderly ladies, for it is run in the same spirit as the London Marathon – taking part is as important as winning.

The Biennale The centenary celebrations of this great international art festival were held in 1995. It now occurs in every odd year, from June to September. The main exhibits are on display in the pavilions of the **Public Gardens** (*see* p.81) but some of the most interesting events take place outside the main venue. Check with the tourist office.

Feast of the Redeemer (Festa del Redentore) Celebrated on the third Sunday of July, this commemorates the end of the plague of 1576, which was marked by the building of the Church of the Redeemer on the Giudecca in 1577 (*see* p.84). A pontoon bridge is built over the Giudecca Canal to allow processions to cross to the church. After religious ceremonies there are various festivities, including fireworks at night.

Fireworks illuminate the Lion of St Mark's Square during the celebrations.

97

Historic Regatta (Regata Storica)
A colourful event, celebrated on the first
Sunday in September, in which richly
decorated historic craft, crewed by men in
period dress, proceed along the Grand
Canal. It is followed by a race between
gondoliers.

The Festival of Salvation (Festa della Salute)
Held on 21 November this commemorates,
in the same way as the Feast of the
Redeemer, the building of the Church of
Our Lady of Salvation after the plague of
1630.

Entertainment and Nightlife
There is little in the way of conventional
nightlife in Venice apart from several
cinemas and some lively bars. If you are a
music lover, however, this is your city. It was,
after all, the home of two of Italy's great
composers: **Monteverdi** was a director of the
choir at St Mark's and **Vivaldi** conducted the
choir of a girls' orphanage, the Ospedale
della Pietà. This was no ordinary orphanage,
for the girls' entire training was in music.

In the 18C, a French visitor remarked:
'Not a single evening goes by without a
concert somewhere. You cannot realize how
crazy the city is about this art.' And it still is.
In addition, visitors accustomed to the hair-
raising prices for opera in Britain are in for a
pleasant surprise. A good seat can be had for
25 000 lire (£10/$16.50) or less.

Doyen of all the theatres was the opera
house, appropriately called **La Fenice**
(*'Phoenix'*), for it was rebuilt after being
burned down in 1831. Verdi's *La Traviata*
had its première here in 1853. Tragically, it
was destroyed again by fire in January 1996,

View over Venice at dusk from the Campanile in St Mark's Square.

but rebuilding is planned. The **Teatro Goldoni** puts on a variety of plays, in addition to Goldoni's (his house in the Calle dei Nomboli is now a museum), and also has music seasons. Concerts are often given in the larger churches: check for programme details and venues in a tourist office.

A goal for most American visitors is the now legendary **Harry's Bar**, Ernest Hemingway's watering hole (in the Calle Vallaresso, near the tourist office). You will need a well-filled wallet, and perhaps one visit to this crowded, noisy bar will be enough, but it is now as much a part of Venice as the Campanile. The bar was founded in 1931 by a bartender, **Giuseppe Cipriani**. Try his own invention, a mixture of champagne and peach juice – the Bellini.

Many visitors, especially Americans, head straight for Harry's Bar.

Food and Drink

Non arat, non seminat, non vidimiat, the mainlanders mocked: 'They don't plough, sow or make wine.' Nevertheless, Venetians eat and drink spectacularly well. The Veneto region produces many famous wines: among the whites, try Soave, Pinot Grigio and sparkling Prosecco; notable reds include Valpolicella, Bardolino and sumptuous Amarone.

Naturally, seafood is abundant and good.

Look for *risotto al mare* (rice with seafood) or *risotto nero* (with squid) among the wealth of fish dishes. Meat-eaters will enjoy *carpaccio* (thin raw beef, a Venetian invention) and *fegato alla veneziana* (liver and onions). Vegetarians have a cornucopia to choose from. A simple Venetian dish is *Risi e bisi* (rice with peas).

Venice can be the most expensive place to eat in Italy. The nearer you are to St Mark's Square the more you will pay – anything up to 12 500 lire (£5/$8) for a cup of coffee in

There are salamis to suit all tastes – ideal for a picnic lunch.

the Piazza itself. For that, however, you are enjoying a unique experience, to the accompaniment of an excellent orchestra. But most restaurants will have a **menu turistico**, a fixed-price meal consisting of a first and second course and a couple of glasses of wine. Reasonably cheap is the **tavola calda** ('hot table'), where you sit up at a bar and there is a limited but good menu. The now universal **pizza** is a good standby, with a glass of wine. A wide variety of the famous Venetian *tramezzini* (sandwiches filled with tuna, asparagus, eggs, zucchini, etc) are served at most bars.

If on a budget, it is worthwhile building up a **picnic** for lunch and spending more in the evening. Grocers (*alimentari*) stock an astonishing range of pickled foods including

This café has unmatched views of St Mark's Basilica.

such delicacies as **anchovies** (*acciughe*),
artichoke hearts (*carciofi*) and a vast range of
fungi. The market stalls near the Rialto will
provide everything you could possibly need
for a splendid picnic.

Music from the orchestra is on the menu at this café on St Mark's Square.

Shopping

Shopping, like eating, is extremely
expensive – but also can be extremely good
value, for the tradition of the individual
Venetian craftsman is still flourishing,
despite the ocean of tourist junk. Again, as
with food, anything bought in and around St
Mark's costs far more.

General shopping is concentrated in the
rather unattractive region known as
Merceria, a chain of streets running from
the Torre dell'Orologio. Many of the open-

air **markets** have stalls selling everything from **shoes** to **antiques**. Ordinary domestic products will be priced, but for antiques and the like it is up to you to decide what you really want to pay.

Pre-eminent among local products is, of course, the world-famous and unique **glass** industry, turning out everything from exquisite wine-glasses to grotesque ornaments. If time permits it is worthwhile going to **Murano**, the heart of the industry, where you can actually see the process and there is a greater range of price and choice. It is inadvisable to accept any tout's offer of a 'free' trip to the island, which will be anything but free when you arrive there.

Carnival masks are also unique to Venice. Dating back to the 17C, the designs are bizarre and usually very eye-catching. They have become so popular that they are now

These market stalls are situated on the Campo Santa Maria Formosa.

Brightly coloured masks are popular souvenirs.

mass-produced, but you can still find well-designed hand-crafted masks at a price.

Lace, too, is a uniquely Venetian product, but it needs an expert eye to detect the difference between machine-made and handmade lace. If you are making a trip to the islands and really want local stuff it is worthwhile shopping in **Burano** where hand-crafted items can be easily found.

Although not cheap, Venice also offers a good range of well-made high quality **looking-glasses**.

THE BASICS

Before You Go

Visitors entering Italy should have a full passport, valid to cover the period in which they will be travelling. No visa is required for members of EU countries or citizens of Eire, the United States, Canada, Australia and New Zealand. No vaccinations are necessary.

Getting There

International flights arrive at Marco Polo Airport from many European destinations, but travellers from further afield may have to fly to another city airport – such as Rome or Milan – and take a connecting flight.

Package tours and charter flights to Venice are both plentiful and popular, and they are available from the UK, Eire and the USA.

Fast train services connect Venice with other major European cities, such as Vienna, Munich and Paris, and from London the Venice–Simplon Orient Express offers a luxury service via Paris. Trains also connect the Channel ports with Venice, although various changes are necessary, and they arrive at the Santa Lucia Station on the Grand Canal.

Coaches regularly leave London for Venice, calling at Paris, Turin, Genoa and Milan en route. Driving to Venice can be an enjoyable exercise if you are not short of time; routes from the east are now limited by the situation in former Yugoslavia, but there are many entry points from the north and north-west.

Arriving

The most memorable way to arrive is by water-bus, and the journey from the airport to St Mark's takes about 30 minutes. A private water taxi costs much more, and it is better to agree a price before setting off so that misunderstandings do not occur.

Public buses run hourly from the airport to Piazzale Roma, the road traffic terminus, and airline buses also meet flights, although these are considerably more expensive. Taxis are also available.

The train station is right on the Grand Canal, and water-buses (*vaporetti*) stop nearby.

Within three days of arriving in Italy, all foreign nationals must register with the police. If you are staying in a hotel, the management will normally attend to this formality, but the visitor is responsible for checking that it has been carried out.

There is no limit on the importation into Italy of tax-paid goods bought in an EU country, provided they are for personal consumption, with the exception of alcohol and tobacco which have fixed limits governing them.

Colourful window boxes brighten a façade.

Accidents and Breakdowns

In case of a breakdown, dial
☎ 116 and the operator will
send an ACI (Italian
Automobile Club) service
vehicle. A red warning triangle
should be placed 50m (55yds)
behind the vehicle, and your
hazard warning lights switched
on. In the event of an accident,
exchange names, addresses
and insurance details. To
contact the police or
ambulance dial ☎ 113. There
are emergency telephones at
1km (0.6 mile) intervals along
the motorways (*autostrade*).

Fully comprehensive
insurance is advisable for
motorists in Italy, and
motoring organizations
recommend that you carry a
green card (obtainable before
you leave), although this is no
longer a legal requirement.

Accommodation

For information before you go
on all aspects of staying in
Venice, refer to the *Michelin
Red Guide Italia*.

Italian hotels are classified
from one to five stars, and
Venice is well supplied with
accommodation in all classes,
including guest houses
(*pensioni*), now all classified as
one-star hotels, and inns
(*locande*). The average double
bedroom with private
bath/shower in a three-star
hotel costs between
132 000 and 204 000 lire
(£50–80 or $80–130); breakfast
is usually extra.

Centrally located hotels are
very much in demand, and it is
advisable to reserve
accommodation well in
advance of your visit,
particularly in the summer, at
Easter or Christmas, and
during Carnival. Hotels
located along the Grand Canal
or near St Mark's can be very
expensive, although prices can
often be negotiated if you are
planning to visit Venice out of
season.

The Tourist Information
Offices at Santa Lucia Station,
St Mark's Square and Piazzale

Roma offer hotel information and a free booking service, and there is a similar service at Marco Polo Airport. The Venice Tourist Board produces an annual list of all hotels, their facilities, and their prices.

The only official YHA hostel in Venice is the Ostello Venezia on the island of Giudecca, at Fondamenta Zitelle 86,☎ 041 5238 211. Student hostels, and sometimes religious institutions, can accommodate young travellers in Venice who are on a tight budget.

There are no camp-sites in Venice but there are plenty on the mainland within easy reach of the city (*see* **Camping**).

For information on accommodation and other aspects of your visit to Venice, contact the offices of the Italian State Tourist Board in your home country (for addresses *see* **Tourist Information Offices**).

Airports *see* **Arriving, p.106**

Babysitters *see* **Children**

Gondolas moored, awaiting hire.

Banks

Banks are open from 8.30am–1.30pm, Monday to Friday, and for one hour in the afternoon, usually 2.45–3.45pm. They are closed at weekends. Tourists can change money at the main railway station and airport, and travellers' cheques and cheques can be changed at most hotels, although this option is best avoided as the rates of exchange are often poor.

Major credit cards may be used at automatic cash dispensers, which can be found at the Banca d'America e d'Italia on Calle Larga XXII Marzo, and the Banca Commerciale d'Italia at Campo San Bartolomeo.

Beaches

Now one of the most fashionable resorts in Europe, much of the beach area at the Lido is privately owned by hotels, and admittance is charged for use of the rest. These offer dressing rooms for hire, lifeguards, and snack bars. A free beach can, however, be found at the Alberoni end of the Lido.

Other accessible – and free – beaches are at Punta Sabbioni, which can be reached by ferry, and the popular resort of Jesolo.

Bicycles

These can be hired at the Lido, both for adults, with optional child seat, and for children.

Breakdowns see Accidents

Buses see Transport

Camping

Venice does not have any camp-sites, but there are plenty within quite easy reach of the city. The nicest – and most expensive – of these are on the Cavallino peninsula, between Jesolo and Punta Sabbioni, reached by vaporetti nos. 12, 14 and 15 from Venice.

Mainland sites are at Maghera, Mestre and Fusina, while the closest is the Camping San Nicolò 65 on the Lido; ☎ 041 5267415. For details of all of the camp-sites around the city, write to the office of the Italian State Tourist Board in your home country (see Tourist Information Offices).

Canal Trips see Excursions

Car Hire

For a city that is completely car-free, Venice is surprisingly well stocked with car-hire agencies, with outlets at the airport, the Piazzale Roma car park, and other points on the mainland. Airlines and tour operators offer fly/drive arrangements, which are often very economical.

Weekly rates with unlimited mileage offer the best deal; these include breakdown service and basic insurance, but you are advised to take out a collision damage waiver and personal accident insurance. The small local firms generally offer the cheapest rates, but they can only be booked locally. Most hire companies restrict hire of cars to drivers over 21.

Drivers must have held their full licence for at least a year. With the exception of Avis, there is an upper age limit of 60–65. Unless paying by credit card a substantial cash deposit is required. Full details of the different hire schemes can be obtained from tourist offices. *See also* **Accidents and Breakdowns**, and **Tourist Information Offices.**

Children

Venice is not perhaps the most obvious place to take children, but there are many things that they will enjoy. Boat trips and rides on gondolas give great pleasure, and glass-blowing is fascinating for all ages.

Children under four not occupying a seat travel free on Italian railways; between the ages of four and 12, they get a reduction of 50 per cent. Those under 1m (3ft 3in) tall also travel free on the water-buses.

Baby food can be bought in the chemist's (*farmacia*) or at supermarkets and grocers, and disposable nappies are equally readily available.

Babysitting can often be arranged by hotels, who keep a list of *bambinaia*, normally local students.

Churches *see* **Religion**

Climate

Spring and autumn can be warm and pleasant times of the year to visit Venice, and during those months light clothes can be worn in the day, with an extra sweater or jacket for the evenings and cooler days. Early spring and late autumn may be cold and damp, however, so bring warm clothes too, just in case. The weather is coldest from mid-November to mid-February.

The summer is normally sweltering, and feels even hotter because of the large numbers of people. There is also the added discomfort of mosquitoes. If you must sightsee during July and August, dress as lightly as possible, but you must remember to cover up shoulders and thighs when visiting churches.

Generally, Venice is quite informal, except during the cold months when Venetians often dress up to go out.

Clothing

Most Italian clothing measurements follow the standard current throughout Europe but differ from those in the UK and the USA. The following are examples:

Dress Sizes

UK	8	10	12	14	16	18
Italy	38	40	42	44	46	48
US	6	8	10	12	14	16

Men's Suits

UK/US	36	38	40	42	44	46
Italy	46	48	50	52	54	56

Men's Shirts

UK/US	14	14.5	15	15.5	16	16.5	17
Italy	36	37	38	39/40	41	42	43

Men's Shoes

UK	7	7.5	8.5	9.5	10.5	11
Italy	41	42	43	44	45	46
US	8	9	9.5	10.5	11.5	12

Women's Shoes

UK	4.5	5	5.5	6	6.5	7
Italy	38	38	39	39	40	40
US	6	6.5	7	7.5	8	8.5

Complaints

Make any complaint at a hotel, shop or restaurant to the manager in a calm manner. For more serious complaints, contact the police (*Polizia*) at the central headquarters (*questura*) on ☎ 5203222, or report your problem to the tourist office (*see* **Tourist Information Offices**). Wherever possible try to establish the cost of something in advance, especially if hiring a gondola, or using a porter at the station.

Consulates

Embassies and consulates can be found at the following addresses:
British Consulate: Palazzo Querini, Accademia, Dorsoduro 1051, Venice. ☎ **522 7207**
Irish Embassy: Largo del Nazareno 3, 00187 Rome. ☎ **06 678 2541**
Australian Embassy: Via Alessandria 215, 00198 Rome. ☎ **06 83 2721**
Canadian Consulate: Via V. Pisani 19, 20124 Milan. ☎ **02 669 7451**
New Zealand Embassy: Via Zara 28, Rome. ☎ **06 440 2928**
United States Consulate: Via Principe Amedeo 2/10, Milan. ☎ **02 29 0351**

Venice takes on a romantic mood through the mist.

Crime

As in many of the world's towns and cities, Venice is a target for pickpockets and petty thieves, although perhaps less so than other European cities popular with tourists. The best advice is to be aware at all times, carry as little money and as few credit cards as possible, and leave any valuables in the hotel safe.

Carry wallets and purses in secure pockets inside your outer clothing, wear body belts, or carry handbags across your body or firmly under your arm. Never leave your car unlocked, and hide away or remove items of value.

If you have anything stolen, report it immediately to the police at the headquarters (*questura*) on ☎ 5203222. Collect a report so that you can make an insurance claim. If your **passport** is stolen, report it to your Consulate or Embassy at once.

Currency *see* Money

Customs and Entry Regulations *see* Arriving, p.106

Disabled Visitors

Venice was not designed with the disabled in mind, and there are many obstructions to their progress in this city of canals, stepped bridges and water-buses. There is wheelchair access on the *vaporetti*, but parts of the city would still appear to be inaccessible to the physically handicapped.

Michelin Red Guide Italia indicates hotels and restaurants with facilities suitable for disabled visitors. A publication called *Venezia per tutti* lists all of those sights and places of interest which can be reached on foot or by *vaporetto*, without having to cross any bridges, plus hotels located on the islands off Venice. For a free copy of this publication, write to: Unità Locale Socio Sanitaria, Dorsoduro 3493, Venice.

However, travellers are strongly recommended to check their particular requirements when making hotel or restaurant reservations.

Driving

There are no cars in the centre of Venice, and the nearest you can get by motor is to the Piazzale Roma. There are multi-storey garages here, and a convenient *vaporetto* landing stage and taxi stand are nearby. Cars can be left in the huge open-air car park on the island of Tronchetto, which is connected by public water-bus to the centre of the city, and by car ferry to the Lido, where you can take cars.

Car parking is also available at Mestre and Fusina, both of which are connected to Venice in the summer months by vaporetto. On the approach into Venice, automatic signs on the motorway indicate the availability of car-parking spaces.

If you are driving through Italy to Venice, make sure that you are familiar with the rules of the road. Remember to drive on the right, and give way to traffic coming from the right.

All the major routes have petrol stations at frequent intervals; they are normally open from 7.30-noon, and 4.00-7.00pm, Monday to Friday, but most are closed on Saturday and Sunday, as well as public holidays; opening hours vary from station to station, and depend on the season. Unleaded petrol is sold, but very few petrol stations accept credit cards.

The following speed limits apply:

Cars and Motorcycles
Motorways: 130kph/80mph
Country roads: 90kph/56mph
Built-up areas: 50kph/31mph

Campers
Motorways: 100kph/62mph
Country roads: 80kph/50mph
Built-up areas: 50kph/31mph

Drivers should carry a full national or international driving licence, and an Italian translation of the licence unless it is a pink European licence; also insurance documents including a green card (no longer compulsory for EU members but strongly recommended), registration papers for the car, and a nationality sticker at its rear.

Headlight beams should be adjusted for right-hand drive, and a red warning triangle must be carried unless there are hazard warning lights on the car; you should also have a spare set of light bulbs. *See also* **Accidents and Breakdowns**.

Dry Cleaning see Laundry

Electric Current
The voltage in Italy is usually 220V. Plugs and sockets are usually round two-pinned ones, and **adaptors** are generally required.

Embassies see Consulates

Emergencies
In an emergency, for **Ambulance, Fire** or **Police** ☎113

Red Cross Ambulance
☎ 523 00 00
Carabinieri ☎ 112
Automobile Club d'Italia (car breakdown) ☎ 116
In cases of dire distress, the Consulate or Embassy might offer limited help.

Etiquette
As in most places in the world, it is considered polite and respectful to cover up decently in churches, museums, and theatres etc. Italians are a courteous people, and although less formal than many other Europeans, greet each other with 'good morning' (*buon giorno*) or 'good evening' (*buona sera*).

Excursions
Tours of Venice's innumerable sights can be made independently, or as part of a guided tour with an English-speaking guide, either on foot or by boat. Excursions of various lengths to the islands and towns of the lagoon are also available, as are trips farther afield; for details ask at the CIT tourist agency in St Mark's Square, or at your hotel. An experienced guide can be hired to take you around Venice, and details of these services can also be found at CIT or your hotel.

Guidebooks *see* Maps

Health
UK nationals should carry a Form E111 (forms available from post offices) which is produced by the Department of Health, and which entitles the holder to free urgent treatment for accident or illness in EU countries. The treatment will have to be paid for in the first instance, but can be reclaimed later.

All foreign nationals are advised to take out comprehensive insurance cover, and to keep any bills, receipts and invoices to support any claim.

Lists of English-speaking doctors can be obtained from hotels, and first aid and medical advice is also available from any pharmacy (*farmacia*), the principal staff of which are very well trained (look out for the green or red cross).

The latter are generally open during normal shopping hours, and lists of those which are open late or on Sundays are displayed at every chemist's shop. First aid (*pronto soccorso*) is available at the main hospital in Venice, next to the church of SS Giovanni e Paolo, ☎ 520717.

Hours *see* Opening Hours

A gondola ride along the quieter canals is a relaxing way of exploring.

Information *see* **Tourist Information Offices**

Language

Many Venetians working in hotels, restaurants and around the main tourist areas speak quite good English, but this can by no means be relied on everywhere. Your efforts to speak Italian will be much appreciated and sometimes essential, and even a few simple words and expressions are often warmly received. A few words and phrases (p.118)

will help you make the most of your stay in Venice.

Laundry

Hotels charge high prices for laundry and dry cleaning, so it is well worthwhile finding a launderette where you can either do your own washing or have it done for you – there is no difference in the price. There is only a handful of laundromats and dry cleaners in Venice, and your hotel receptionist will tell you where the nearest ones are.

Yes/no: Sì/no [see/noh]
Please/thank you: Per favore/grazie [pair favoray/gratsiay]
Do you speak English? Parla inglese? [parla inglaysay?]
How much is it? Quanto costa? [kwanto costa?]
The bill, please: Il conto, per favore [eel conto, pair favoray]
Excuse me: Mi scusi [mee scoozi]
I'd like a stamp: Vorrei un francobollo [vóray oon francobollo]
Do you accept travellers' cheques? Accetta travellers' cheques? [achetta...]
I don't understand: Non capisco [nohn capisco]
Good morning: Buon giorno [bwon jyorno]
Good afternoon/evening: Buona sera [bwohna saira]

Lost Property

Lost property is quite likely to turn up again in Venice, so try retracing your steps and asking at the last places you have been to. Venetians are inherently honest, and if they find any property they are likely to hand it to an official.

If you are unlucky and your property cannot be readily found, try the lost property office – Ufficio all'Economato, Calle Corner Piscopia o Loredan 4134, near the Rialto Bridge. The airport and railway station have their own lost property offices, and if something goes missing in your hotel, check with the front desk and hotel security.

Anything lost on the vaporetti may turn up at the Objects Found Office (*Oggetti rinvenuti*) of ACTV, the water transport agency, at St Angelo Stop (No. 9) on the Grand Canal.

Should you lose any travel documents, contact the police, and in the event of a passport going missing, inform your Embassy or Consulate immediately (*see* **Consulates**). Lost or stolen travellers' cheques and credit cards should be reported immediately to the issuing company, with a list of numbers, and the police should also be informed.

Maps

A full range of maps and guides is published by Michelin. Map no 988 *Italy* and no 429 *Italy (Northeast)* will help you plan your routes when travelling through Italy. The *Green Guide Venice* (publication mid-1996) contains detailed information on what to see and where to go in Venice. *Green Guide Italy* includes excellent information for all of Italy, including Venice. Information on restaurants and accommodation can be found in the *Michelin Red Guide Italia*.

Medical Care *see* Health

Money

The monetary unit of Italy is the Italian *lira*, and notes are issued in denominations of 1 000, 2 000, 5 000, 10 000, 50 000 and 100 000 *lire*. Coins are of 50, 100, 200 and 500 *lire*. All major credit cards, travellers' cheques and Eurocheques are accepted in many shops, restaurants, hotels, and some large motorway petrol stations outside the city.

There are no restrictions on the amount of currency visitors can take into Italy, but perhaps the safest way to carry large amounts of money is in travellers' cheques, which are widely accepted and exchanged. Bureaux de change are found at the airport, the railway station, and around the main tourist areas

of St Mark's and the Rialto Bridge; banks also change money and travellers' cheques (*see also* **Banks**).

Exchange rates vary, so it pays to shop around; usually the rate offered by the bank will be better than that given at the currency exchange offices (*cambio*). You are not advised to pay hotel bills in foreign currency or with travellers' cheques since the hotel's exchange rate is likely to be the highest of all.

Newspapers

Foreign newspapers and magazines can be bought from newsagents near St Mark's Square and the Rialto Bridge, as well as at the airport and the railway station. They are usually a day late, except for the *International Herald Tribune* which is published in Paris, and contains the latest stock market news from America as well as world news.

The two local papers, *Gazzettino* and *Nuova Venezia*, provide a calendar of events and current information.

Opening Hours

Shops are open from 8.30/9.00am–12.30pm, and from 3.30/4.00–7.30/8.00pm. Most shops close all day on Sunday, except those which are

Kiosk selling souvenirs and postcards.

geared to tourists, and some are closed on Monday morning or Wednesday afternoon.

Museums and galleries operate their own very idiosyncratic hours and it is impossible to generalize; ask at the tourist office.

Post offices open from 8.30am–1.30pm, Monday to Saturday.

Churches open from about 7.00am–noon, and from 4.00–7.00pm. (*See also* **Tourist Information Offices** and **Banks**)

Photography

Good-quality film and camera equipment are readily available but expensive in Venice, and although there are facilities for fast processing throughout the city, this is usually much cheaper at home. Before taking photographs in museums and art galleries, it is wise to check with staff, as photography is usually restricted in these places.

Police

The *carabinieri* deal with serious crime in the city (☎ 112); the *polizia* handle general crime, including lost passports and theft reports for insurance claims (☎ 5203222). The *polizia stradale* deal with traffic problems outside the city.

The Venice police are rarely to be seen, but when they are around they are courteous to foreign tourists.

Post Offices

The main post office in Venice is at Fondaco dei Tedeschi, near the Rialto Bridge, and is open from 8.30am–6.45pm, Monday to Saturday. It provides a 24-hour international telephone service, fax and telex, as well as *poste restante* facilities (letters should be addressed to the surname (underlined), c/o Fermo Posta, Posta Centrale, Rialto, Venice). Those collecting *poste restante* mail should bring their passport with them.

The other central post office in Calle Larga dell'Ascensione, close to St Mark's Square, opens from 8.30am–1.30pm, Monday to Saturday.

Stamps are sold only by post offices, and tobacconists which display a dark blue and white 'T' sign.

Public Holidays

New Year's Day: 1 January
Epiphany: 6 January
Easter Monday
Liberation Day: 25 April
Labour Day: 1 May
Assumption Day: 15 August
All Saints: 1 November
Immaculate Conception:
    8 December
Christmas Day and Boxing
    Day: 25 and 26 December

Public Transport *see* Transport

Religion

Most people living in Venice are Catholic, and the churches celebrate mass in Italian every Sunday. Several masses are said at St Mark's Basilica (☎ 5225697) every day, except on Saturday when there is only one evening mass. Confession is heard every day in several languages, including English.

Other churches in Venice include:
St George's Anglican Church, Dorsoduro, Campo S Vio; ☎ 5200571.

Evangelical Lutheran, Cannaregio, Campo SS Apostoli, 4443.

Greek Orthodox, Castello Ponte dei Greci 3412.

Jewish Synagogue, Ghetto Vecchio 1228; ☎ 715012.

Smoking

Smoking is banned in churches, museums and art galleries, and is discouraged in restaurants. There are separate non-smoking compartments in trains. **Tobacconists** (*tabacchi*), which carry a sign with a white 'T' inside a dark blue rectangle, sell the major international brands of cigarettes. These are also on sale in bars and restaurants.

Stamps see Post Offices

Taxis see Transport

Telephones

Venice is very well off for public telephones, which are sited around the city and in most cafés and bars. They take either telephone cards to the value of 5 000 or 10 000 lire, sold at newsagents and tobacconists, or 100, 200 and 500 lire coins; some also take *gettoni*, telephone tokens.

To make an international call from Italy, dial 001 for US and Canada, 00 44 for UK, 00 61 for Australia, and 00 64 for New Zealand. Cheap rates apply between 11.00pm and 8.00am, Monday to Saturday, and all day Sunday.

International calls can best be made from the offices of the Telecom, which are next to the main post office at the Rialto Bridge, or at the station and Piazzale Roma. You can dial direct from here, and pay for the call afterwards. Credit card calls and reversed charge calls can also be made here.

Long-distance phone calls from hotels are very expensive, although very convenient if money is no problem.

Time Difference

Italian standard time is GMT plus one hour. Italian summer time begins on the last weekend in March, when the clocks go forward an hour (the same day as British Summer Time), and ends on the last weekend in September, when the clocks go back (one month before BST ends).

Tipping

A service charge of 10 or 15 per cent is usually included in the bill at hotels and restaurants in Italy, but a tip (minimum amount 1 000 lire) is also given where the service has been particularly pleasing. Check the bill to see if service has been included.

Usherettes who show you to your seat in a cinema or theatre should receive a tip, as well as hotel porters, airport and railway porters, and lavatory attendants. Taxi drivers and tour guides will expect about 10 per cent, but do not feel that you must tip a gondolier if you have already paid a small fortune for his services.

Toilets

There are public conveniences at the railway station, the airport and some museums, but otherwise they are quite thin on the ground. Use the toilets in bars and restaurants, which may be shared by the sexes, or separate for women (*signore*) and men (*signori*).

Tourist Information Offices

The Italian State Tourist Board (ENIT) is a good source of information on what is happening in Venice. The information offices in the city are staffed by speakers of English as well as other foreign languages, and have information on timetables, accommodation and programmes of events.

The main office is at St Mark's Square, but there is also an office at the railway station, and one at Piazzale Roma (this only gives out information on accommodation).

The Tourist Board also has offices in many countries, including the following English-speaking ones:

Typical canal-corner scene.

UK: 1 Princes Street, London W1R 8AY.
☎ 0171 408 1254

USA: 630 Fifth Avenue, Suite 1565, New York, NY 10111.
☎ 212 245 4822

Canada: 1 Place Ville-Marie, Suite 1914, Montreal, Quebec, H3B 3M9.
☎ 514 866 7667/8/9

Australia and New Zealand: ENIT, c/o Alitalia, Orient

Overseas Building, Suite 202, 32 Bridge Street, Sydney, NSW 2000.
☎ 2 271 308

Eire: 47 Merrion Square, Dublin 2.
☎ 01 766397

A free publication offering practical information for English- and Italian-speaking tourists is available from the tourist office: ask for *Un Ospite di Venezia,* which comes out fortnightly between April and October, and monthly in the intervening months.

Tours see **Excursions**

Transport

You can quite easily walk everywhere in Venice, but the water-buses (*vaporetti*) offer a frequent and efficient transport system; they mainly travel up and down the Grand Canal, but they also follow a circuitous route around the edge of the city, and run to and from the islands. They display route numbers.

The *vaporetti* most frequently used by tourists run every ten minutes during the day and early evening, and much less often at night; after about 1am it is necessary either to walk or to take a water taxi.

Get hold of a plan of the various routes, so that you can see which number *vaporetto* you need. Each landing stage is numbered, and you can buy your ticket from the vendor at the landing stage. Prices are dearer for the more direct

Gondola tours can be expensive, so you should always agree a price first.

services, and cheaper for those that stop at every stage.

Water taxis have a fixed rate, in theory, but do not be surprised if this changes every time you take a ride. They are not a cheap form of transport, and there are surcharges for luggage and night rides, to name but two. To call a water taxi, ☎ 5232326 or 5222303.

Gondolas are seen as a must for many tourists, but they are very expensive, and even the officially set rates are often wildly exceeded. The minimum hire time is 50 minutes, and you are advised to agree a price for your ride before setting off. The tourist publication *Un Ospite di Venezia*, available from the tourist offices, lists the official rates; these are higher after 8pm.

The Santa Lucia railway station on the Grand Canal is always busy, and it is recommended that you arrive in plenty of time for your train if you have not made a reservation. There are several different ways of getting reductions on rail travel, and details can be obtained from the Italian State Tourist Board in your own country, or any travel agent.

TV and Radio

Vatican Radio broadcasts English-language religious news programmes at various times of the day. During the tourist season the Italian state radio and television network (RAI) broadcasts news in English on the radio at 10.00am, Monday to Saturday, and at 9.30am on Sunday.

Shortwave radio reception is very good in Venice, and British, Canadian and American programmes can be easily heard, especially at night. RAI television broadcasts only in Italian.

Vaccinations see Before You Go, p.106

Water Quality

Venetian water is perfectly safe to drink, unless the tap has a sign saying *acqua non potabile* (not for drinking). It is usual to order a bottle of water, *acqua minerale*, with meals.

What to Wear see Climate

Youth Hostels see Accommodation

INDEX

This index includes entries in English (where used in the guide) and in Italian (*italics*).

INDEX